A RIGHT TO EXIST

Whose Rights Are Right?

JOHN JEFFREY

iUniverse books may be ordered through booksellers or by contacting:

iUniverse
1663 Liberty Drive
Bloomington, IN 47403
www.iuniverse.com
1-800-Authors (1-800-288-4677)

Because of the dynamic nature of the Internet, any web addresses or links contained in this book may have changed since publication and may no longer be valid. The views expressed in this work are solely those of the author and do not necessarily reflect the views of the publisher, and the publisher hereby disclaims any responsibility for them.

Any people depicted in stock imagery provided by Thinkstock are models, and such images are being used for illustrative purposes only. Certain stock imagery © Thinkstock.

ISBN: 978-1-4917-7577-6 (sc)
ISBN: 978-1-4917-7576-9 (e)

Library of Congress Control Number: 2015915644

Print information available on the last page.

iUniverse rev. date: 11/03/2015

To the two greatest women in my life. My mother, the late Mrs. Lena Mae Jeffrey, from whom I learned most of life's greatest lessons about how to live and conduct myself as a respectable man. Her teachings have molded and shaped me into the man I am today, and they continue to guide me even now. Also to my loving wife, Anna, who has been a great inspiration and support to me—not only during the writing of this book but from the time we said, "I do."

Contents

Introduction

This book is about the many different types of rights of citizens, mostly in America, and how these rights affect our lives and our futures. The American public is crying out to be heard on matters such as LGBT rights, environmental rights, animal rights, abortion rights, and more, most of which society wants to place under the umbrella of *civil rights*. This book looks at where rights began, the long struggle of black civil rights, and what actually constitutes a right. All references to the Bible are from the authorized King James Version. Court documents, government statistics, and books are referenced in many cases.

"I have a right" is probably the most commonly heard phrase in America, and it is becoming more widely used around the world. Everybody claims his or her right to do and say as he or she pleases. Everyone harps on his or her constitutional right of free speech, using it as an excuse to say anything, no matter how offensive. The only problem is a failure to consider the other person's rights. If you have a right, then so does everyone else. When your right infringes upon someone else's rights, where will the line be drawn to determine whose rights get precedence?

The Declaration of Independence states that every American has certain unalienable rights that are given by the Creator, among which are life, liberty, and the pursuit of happiness. People have taken the idea of rights being guaranteed by the Constitution to mean the right to do whatever they want (whenever they want) and say whatever they want. They think it's legal to do so. We have the law, and then we also have the spirit, or the common sense or intent, of the law.

The Founding Fathers, as they are so often called set up America's system of government. It is a government for the people, by the people, and of the people. The people have a say in who governs them, and the people have a voice on issues. It has taken time for the United States of America to actually become united under the Constitution, which is the supreme law for the nation. Before this complete uniting of the states, the country was divided over issues, mostly the issue of slavery, which caused the war between the North and South. However, with the current state of events and cries for everyone's rights to be respected, will the system survive?

After the Civil War, President Abraham Lincoln issued his famous Gettysburg Address. In his speech, the president stated, "This nation, under God, shall have a new birth of freedom and that government of the people, by the people, for the people, shall not perish from the earth." Mr. Lincoln said the "right of the people," which was an inclusive statement, encompassing all people of America—not just a collective few. Even after the Civil War, which was fought over slaves having freedom and constitutional rights, division continued about those rights. People have to come to a conclusion about what rights really are and which rights people are entitled to under the Constitution.

Today, the cry for rights goes further than race. It is becoming increasingly common for people to cry for the right to do or say something that is offensive to others and expect no repercussions or backlash. Most of the rights people are crying out to be heard on are actually personal preferences and not rights.

Most people seem to have confused personal preferences with rights. Furthermore, they feel that if they are not allowed those personal preferences, somehow their rights under the Constitution are being violated.

The Constitution guarantees us the right to life, the right to pursue happiness, and the right to be free. Nothing is mentioned or alluded to about personal preferences or desires. Just like with the Bible, people misinterpret the Constitution for their own personal benefit. They twist or attempt to turn the words around to suit themselves.

The Constitution was written to include God and our moral and civil laws, for the most part, were based on the Ten Commandments. God's law was used to govern society, and for the most part, it still does. Everything else is becoming questionable. Mine or yours—whose rights are right?

Chapter 1

Civil Rights, over 100 years of struggle

The Civil War was fought over slaves' rights to be free and be treated as all other human beings as the Constitution declared, which is to have the same liberty as every other American. One hundred years after the Civil War and the freedom of the slaves, black people were still fighting for their constitutional rights. In many cases, their lives were taken from them unjustly—without any recourse from society or the government. Due process of law did not appear to apply to America's black citizens.

They had to fight for the right to pursue happiness through better employment, better benefits, and the right to be treated fairly. They wanted the right to use the same restrooms, eat in the same restaurants, and stay in the same hotels. Many other privileges were reserved only for whites. Most of these unfair practices were happening in the South, but the North was not without its prejudices. Being denied these rights actually defamed black people and made them appear as less than other human beings in the eyes of many. Human beings are human beings regardless to what they look like or what color skin they have. They all walk upright, have the same facial parts, and have the same internal organs.

Blacks had to fight for the right of equal protection under the law, which was denied them in many instances. They were not allowed to serve on juries for many years and were denied trials by their peers. The right to pursue happiness through employment is an example.

For the most part, many qualified people were denied positions and decent pay simply because of the color of their skin. In his "I Have a Dream" speech, Martin Luther King Jr. spoke of seeing the day when black people would be judged not by the color of their skin but by the content of the character. This, in part, is what the original civil rights movement was about. It was a movement that started after Reconstruction and has continued to the present day.

Many laws were passed during the civil rights era. Many laws were overturned, and many were not enforced. Dred Scott fought for his freedom in the courts of the United States. His citizenship was not recognized even though he was born in America. He fought for the right to exist as a free man, arguing the point that he had lived most of his life in states where slavery was illegal. He lost his case after many appeals. The ruling stated that black people were inferior to whites and were not considered citizens by the Constitution. But a man is a man regardless of his race or color, so it was white Americans at the time giving their interpretation of the Constitution.

In one of his many meetings with President John F. Kennedy, Dr. Martin Luther King Jr. asked if the Constitution meant what it said, referring to the clause of all men being endowed with unalienable rights given to them by their Creator. His point was if the Constitution says it, then America should abide by it and allow black people to have the same rights as every other citizen of the United States.

After Reconstruction, the Thirteenth Amendment abolished slavery in the United States, being passed by the Senate on April 8, 1864, and the House on January 31, 1865. President Abraham Lincoln approved it and sent it to the state legislatures for ratification. The states ratified the Thirteenth Amendment on December 6, 1865. This amendment to the Constitution provides that neither slavery nor involuntary servitude—except where the party shall have been duly convicted—shall exist within the United States or any place subject to its jurisdiction. The Thirteenth Amendment was passed at the end of the Civil War, which was fought about whether slavery was right or wrong. This amendment—along with the Fourteenth Amendment and the Fifteenth Amendment—expanded civil rights for black Americans.

Passing legislation is one thing, and implementing it is a horse of a completely different color.

President Lincoln issued the Emancipation Proclamation on January 1, 1863, freeing the slaves and proclaiming that the executive government, military, and naval service shall recognize and maintain the freedom of the slaves. On July 9, 1868, the Fourteenth Amendment granted citizenship to all persons born or naturalized in the United States:

> No state shall make or enforce any law that will abridge the privileges or immunities of citizens of the United States; nor shall any state deprive any person of life, liberty, or property, without due process of law; nor deny to any person within its jurisdiction the equal protection of the laws.

The Civil War brought all the states together under the Constitution. States became subject to the same federal laws of the United States Constitution. In the South, most states ignored the Fourteenth Amendment, eventually passing Jim Crow laws to support their beliefs or prejudices. At the time of the amendment, there were only thirty-seven states in the union. The Fourteenth Amendment passed with the twenty-eight states needed and became part of the supreme law of the land.

The Fifteenth Amendment granted black people the right to vote. "The right of citizens of the United States to vote shall not be denied or abridged by the United States or by any State on account of race, color, or previous condition of servitude." It further stated, "The Congress shall have the power to enforce this article by appropriate legislation."

The new amendments gave black people their just and due rights that the Constitution of the United States had already granted. The battle for these guaranteed rights has lasted longer than the Civil War for black people. Laws benefiting black people were not always enforced.

Many setbacks would be experienced over the next hundred

years, mostly in Southern states that made their own laws to keep black people from receiving their constitutional rights. In the 1890s, steps were taken by whites to ensure white supremacy. Literacy tests and grandfather clauses were instituted for the right to vote. They were written into the constitutions of many Southern states.

States have the right to have their own constitutions, but they are not supposed to conflict with the national Constitution, which is the higher law. At the time, Southern states pretty much did what they wanted, and nobody appeared to be concerned enough to get things changed. Those states also had great representation in Congress and the Senate.

Many civil rights organizations would rise up and fight to secure the rights given to black people through the Constitution and the Thirteenth, Fourteenth, and Fifteenth Amendments. The nations oldest is the NAACP, which was founded on February 12, 1909. The founders were Mary White Ovington and Oswald Garrison Villard, actual descendants of abolitionists, William English Walling, Dr. Henry Moscowitz, W. E. B. DuBois, Ida B. Wells, and Mary Church Terrell.

The NAACP was patterned after Mr. DuBois's Niagara Movement, which began in 1905. Its goal was to secure for all people the rights guaranteed in the Thirteenth, Fourteenth, and Fifteenth Amendments, which promised an end to slavery, the equal protection of the law, and voting rights. Even though the Constitution declared it, black people continually had to fight to receive their rights.

Other important civil rights organizations were the Brotherhood of Sleeping Car Porters (BSCP), organized by A. Philip Randolph in 1925. This organization was instrumental to earning civil rights for black people. The BSCP was the first African-American labor union to sign a collective-bargaining agreement with a major US corporation. It is now known as the Transportation Communication International Union.

The Civil Rights Act of 1875 passed by a vote of 162–99. Senator Charles Summer of Massachusetts introduced the act in 1870. Its original form outlawed racial discrimination in juries, schools, transportation, and public accommodations. Like many other legislative bills, the wording was changed in order to make it acceptable enough to pass in the midst of a growing population that embraced segregation. Seven black representatives argued in favor of the bill, giving personal accounts of discrimination, but they received no sympathy as their testimonies fell on deaf ears. The bill did pass after all references to equal and integrated education were stripped, and the law did not have any power or lasting effects. It died completely when the Supreme Court struck it down in 1883, giving black people another setback.

The Supreme Court stated that the Fourteenth Amendment did not give Congress the authority to prevent discrimination by private individuals. In 1887, Florida passed a law requiring railways to provide "separate accommodations for white and colored races." Mississippi, Texas, and other states soon followed suit.

Louisiana passed the Separate Car Act in 1890, which mandated racial segregation of all railroad passengers. Homer Plessy's skin was light enough to pass for white, and he purchased a ticket for the white section. On the railway car, he identified himself as black. He was arrested and found guilty of violating the act. He appealed the decision, and the Louisiana Supreme Court upheld the lower court's ruling. When the case went to the Supreme Court, Plessy's side argued that the act violated the Thirteenth and Fourteenth Amendments. The Supreme Court issued a ruling that denied Plessy's challenge to the law. Justice Henry Billings Brown argued that as long as the separate facilities were equal, they did not violate the Fourteenth Amendment's guarantee of equal protection under the law. Judge John Marshall Harlan was the only dissenter:

> The white race deems itself to be the dominant race in this country. And so it is, in prestige, in achievements, in education, in wealth, and in power. So, I doubt not, it will continue to be for all time, if it remains true to its great heritage and holds fast to the principles of constitutional liberty. But in the view of the Constitution, in the eye of the law, there is in this country no superior, dominant, ruling class of citizens. There is no caste here. Our Constitution is

color-blind and neither knows nor tolerates classes among citizens. In respect of civil rights, all citizens are equal before the law. The humblest is the peer of the most powerful. The law regards man as man and takes no account of his surroundings or of his color when his civil rights as guaranteed by the supreme law of the land are involved.

From his dissent, Judge John Harlan appears to be a wise, fair, honest, thoughtful man. He was ahead of his time. Judge Harlan stated that the white race was the dominant race in the United States, but he doubted that it would continue to be that way. America was built upon welcoming all races, but that has not always included black people. Immigrants from almost every nation have come to America or attempted to come for the freedom the United States offers. People come to America to take advantage of our education system. Some of them return to their native lands and serve their own people; others remain and become naturalized citizens. US law states that those who are born in America are automatically citizens. However, even noncitizens visiting America have rights; some have diplomatic immunity, and others receive benefits that should only be for citizens.

With the passage of the Civil Rights Act of 1964, black Americans began to experience changes in the way they were treated and served. President John F. Kennedy first suggested this act to Congress in a speech on June 11, 1963. The president asked for legislation that would give all Americans the right to be served in public facilities, including hotels, restaurants, theaters, and retail stores. Jim Crow laws had eliminated these rights and benefits throughout the country, mostly in the South.

President Kennedy's bill included provisions to ban discrimination, but unfortunately for the black community, the thirty-fifth president of the United States would be assassinated before the civil rights act was signed into law. History seemed to be repeating itself for America's black citizens. When victory appeared to be on the horizon for black people, another setback would usually show its ugly head. This seemed to be a common occurrence for the black race.

Whenever presidential leaders spoke up for them or attempted to pass legislation to support their cause, they were either assassinated or overruled by Congress. Others became silent to save their own political careers. The proposed legislation by President Kennedy was not a total fix, but—as with other legislation before it—it was a start. It certainly was not the first civil rights act passed to help the black community. President Kennedy proposed it after a great speech to the American people. He appealed to their collective conscience about racism against black people.

The president appealed to white Americans after the turmoil in Birmingham, Alabama, in April 1963. News coverage showed city policemen turning attack dogs loose on black teenagers and fireman spraying hoses at people. This happened after Dr. Martin Luther King Jr. and other civil rights leaders were arrested for organizing a march for better conditions for black people in the city. While these black leaders were in jail, students continued to protest. The news footage of the incident was shown around the world, and it continues to be shown every year around the Martin Luther King Jr. holiday. The abuse was so graphic that it caused the president of the United States to be moved to action.

Presidents in the past had been reluctant to get too deeply involved in race relations. But this one fell directly on President John Kennedy's plate. The president's speech concerning the black experience and present conditions was so moving that it brought tears to the eyes of many people. He addressed the black situation in great detail and noted that the entire world was watching America.

Mr. Kennedy noted how people of many different backgrounds and nationalities founded America. That is the great principle that continues to be espoused to this day. That principle is that all men are created equal, and when someone takes away one individual's rights, everyone's rights are threatened. The president went into great detail, addressing the Negro condition in America. Stating, that they may have obtained freedom from slavery, but it appears that the American Negro was still not free. During that time, black Americans could not attend amusements parks, eat in public restaurants, or live in the same hotels as whites. The incidents in Birmingham prompted the president's speech to the nation and his legislation to Congress in 1963.

It all started on April 3, 1963, when Dr. Martin Luther King Jr. arrived in Birmingham with the Southern Christian Leadership Conference (SCLC)and joined forces with the Alabama Christian Movement for Human Rights (ACMHR). Dr. King and other adult leaders were sent to jail for violating an anti-protest injunction. They were kept in solitary confinement and denied any phone calls. In an effort to continue the campaign, SCLC organizer James Bezel proposed using students in the march. They seemed to have no other choice if the march and protest were to continue. Some of the adults were afraid of losing their jobs, but allowing the young people to get involved seemed like a good idea since discrimination affected them also. At first, Dr. King was reluctant, but he eventually agreed. The march proved to be successful, but the entire nation was able to see the abuse leveled on the students in their peaceful march.

Under order of Eugene "Bull" Conner, the police and firefighters attacked the students. The whole world was watching as the incident was replayed on national television. On May 10, an agreement was reached between civil rights negotiators and white business owners. Signs that showed white people or black people only were taken down from restrooms and water fountains. Lunch counters were desegregated, and a program to upgrade Negro employment was launched.

Things appeared to be changing, but not everyone was happy. Rioting broke out on May 12 after the bombing of the A. G. Gaston Hotel where black people had met for their integration campaign. Reverend A. D. King, younger brother of Dr. Martin Luther King Jr. and pastor of the First Baptist Church of Ensley, Alabama, had his house bombed. Many thought the Ku Klux Klan did the bombings as it had so often before. Birmingham was nicknamed "Bombingham" in newspapers around the country. As far away as Japan, images of violence were on the front pages. On September 15, 1963, four young black girls were killed in a bombing at the Sixteenth Street Baptist Church.

Before the Birmingham incident, Dr. Martin Luther King was in solitary confinement in Birmingham. He read in the newspaper that clergymen were calling for calm. They also criticized Dr. King for the timing of the April 1963 march. Dr. King's response to the white clergymen was later known as *Letter from a Birmingham Jail*. The letter was written on the edges of the newspaper that criticized King, pieces of scrap paper from an inmate, and pads left by his attorneys. King's lawyer smuggled the letter out of jail.

People thought Dr. King's *Letter from a Birmingham Jail* would be published in the *New York Times*, one of America's most prominent newspapers, but only *The Christian Century, The Atlantic Monthly,* and *The New Leader* published it.

The letter from Martin Luther King Jr. and the speech by President John F. Kennedy were moving and to the point. They honestly addressed the issues and conditions of the time.

Martin Luther King Jr.'s marches and the civil rights movement were about peacefully marching and protesting to receive the rights guaranteed by the Constitution. Black people fought and spoke up for civil rights long before Reverend King. White people and people of other races protested with black people and worked to help the cause. One such person was Pernell Roberts who portrayed Adam cartwright on *Bonanza*. He was born in Waycross, Georgia, and became an outspoken advocate for civil rights. He marched with Dr. King in the historic 1965 march from Selma to Montgomery, Alabama. There were many white sympathizers in the civil rights struggle. From the time of slavery to the sixties, many paid with their lives. This support helped black people receive their constitutional rights.

Dr. Martin Luther King's campaign was regarded as a campaign of peace. He felt that it would be the best way to spread the message about racial injustice. Dr. King helped bring racial injustice into the view of the whole world, especially when ill treatment and injustices were caught on film. Dr. King helped bring racial injustice into the view of the whole world, especially when ill treatment and injustices were caught on film.

The abuse of the peaceful marchers struck a nerve in some people. America began to wake up. In 1964, Dr. King was awarded the Nobel Peace Prize. In his acceptance speech, Dr. King tried to take the focus off of himself as an individual. He wanted the world to focus on the struggle of black people in general, especially those fighting and struggling for their constitutional rights.

On February 12, 1968, black garbage workers went on strike in Memphis. They were protesting poor working conditions and the neglect and abuse of black workers. T. O. Jones, a black union organizer, led more than 1,100 of the union's 1,300 workers. The president of the American Federation of State, County, and Municipal Employees, Jerry Wurf, supported him. The black strikers slogan was: "I Am a Man." They felt that the conditions that they were forced to work under were inhumane. The strike started when two black sanitation workers were crushed to death by a malfunctioning garbage truck during a heavy rainstorm on February 1, 1968. On the same day, twenty-two black sewer workers were sent home without pay in a separate weather-related incident; their white supervisors were retained with pay.

On February 22, 1968, Memphis sanitation workers and their supporters organized a sit-in, in front of the city council. The city council voted to recognize the union and recommended a wage increase for the garbage workers. Mayor Henry Loeb rejected the council's vote, stating that he alone had the power or authority to recognize the union. Loeb was the son of Jewish-German immigrants who had migrated from Germany to Memphis. He was a self-described segregationist. A person with his family's background of racial experience should understand persecution and rejection of the right to exist. Even though his family came to America before the Holocaust, it would seem sensible for him to reject racism, but he did just the opposite by embracing white supremacy.

While in Memphis to support the black garbage workers strike Dr. King was assassinated on April 4, 1968, at the Lorraine Motel on his way to dinner at the home of Samuel "Billy" Kyles. After the assassination, a local minister organized the Community on the move for equality. (Come) Reverend James Lawson went on the radio and asked for calm in Memphis.

Mayor Loeb called for the state police and the National Guard and ordered a 7:00 p.m. curfew. Mayor Loeb had often used the police and the National Guard for sit-ins or peaceful marches during the strike period. In most cases, especially in Southern states, black people were denied their constitutional right of freedom to assemble and petition the government, even though they were peaceful. When black people protested, it was considered against the law. In many cases, they were met with force.

After the death of Dr. King, President Lyndon Johnson sent his undersecretary of labor to Memphis to negotiate an end to the strike. On April 8, Dr. King's widow, Coretta Scott King, led forty-two thousand people, SCLC leaders, and union leaders in a silent march through Memphis in memory of Dr. King's death. In a deal that was finally reached on April 16, the city council recognized the union and guaranteed better wages.

The Voting Rights Act of 1964 was intended to outlaw discriminatory practices in voting that were used widely in the South. Prior to its passage, qualified black voters had to pass literacy tests in order to register to vote and pay poll taxes they couldn't afford. The South often used these practices to prevent black people from voting. President Lyndon B. Johnson signed the civil rights act and the voting rights act into law. These would not have been necessary if the Constitution had been obeyed and followed, giving black people their constitutional rights.

In most cases, the civil rights movement accomplished its goals. It has been a long battle (about one hundred years) from Reconstruction to the death of Dr. Martin Luther King Jr with America coming a long way since Reconstruction. Many discriminatory practices have been done away with. The first black president, Barack Obama, was elected in November 2008. While people can hope, they should not expect to get rid of all discrimination. Discrimination deals with the hearts and minds of people. If people choose to hate, nobody can stop them. It cannot be properly legislated because legislation cannot change people's hearts. However, the law helps fight discriminatory practices, which cannot be done openly without some type of recourse. While the civil rights movement dealt basically with the rights of black people.

Many whites and Jews were involved in the movement and supported black people in their cause. Some people think that many of the organizations that were necessary and beneficial during the civil rights movement are probably no longer needed—or need to be modernized because times have changed. People have to change with the times or remain stuck in the past.

Civil rights organizations fight to preserve the constitutional rights of all people. Even though civil rights organizations fought to get black people the rights they have today, they need to continue to fight to help maintain those rights

Prior to Kennedy and Johnson, other presidents worked to overturn injustices against black people and further the cause of civil rights. However, most presidents were reluctant to get involved with civil rights because it could have meant the end of their political careers, and black civil rights had never been a popular issue. The majority of white America—Republicans and Democrats alike—had been against it for generations. That was why it took so long to get anything accomplished.

Whenever there seemed to be victory in the form of legislation, it was usually overturned or watered down, holding black people back in their quest for equality. Until the 1960's the Republican Party mostly fought for the nation's black citizens receiving their constitutional rights. Now it appears to be the Democratic party. When the civil rights march in Washington was announced, President John Kennedy feared a backlash. There had never been a march of that magnitude (250,000 people). Most presidents didn't want to deal with what was happening on Kennedy's watch.

Most presidents who were involved in the civil rights movement personally sympathized with black people in their struggles, but they were forced to get involved through the passing of legislation or some great tragedy in society. During the civil rights march in Washington, a coalition of many civil rights organizations came together. The organizers were James Farmer of the Congress of Racial

Equality, Martin Luther King Jr. of the Southern Christian Leadership Conference, John Lewis of the Student Nonviolent Coordinating Committee, A. Philip Randolph of the Brotherhood of Sleeping Car Porters, Roy Wilkins of the National Association for the Advancement of Colored People (NAACP), and Whitney Young Jr. of the National Urban League.

During his second term, President Dwight Eisenhower was force to get into the civil rights issue. When the Little Rock Nine (nine black students) began their entrance into Central High School, they were met with great resistance by whites. In 1957 Central High School in Little Rock, Arkansas, was integrated. The Supreme Court had ruled in 1954 that segregation in public schools was unconstitutional. President Eisenhower did not particularly like the court's ruling because he refused to endorse it. He also avoided commenting on the ruling in public, but he was obligated to enforce the law. His silence encouraged resistance by many whites; they organized white citizen's council groups across the South to protest integration. Arkansas Governor Orval Faubus called the Arkansas National Guard to keep the nine students from entering the school. The incident quickly gained national attention. A popular photo was flashed across the front pages of almost every newspaper in the country. The photo showed a black girl leaving the school with an angry white mob shouting racial slurs behind her. The photo is shown almost every year when the issue of civil rights comes up.

President Eisenhower federalized the Arkansas National Guard, which meant they were taken from the control of Governor Faubus, and commanded them to return to their fort. Eisenhower dispatched the 101st Airborne Infantry to Central High to give the students entrance into the school, and the infantry remained there throughout the school year.

Regardless of how people feel about going into situations, they must be credited for their actions and successes. President Eisenhower is credited with taking charge and using his executive power over the governor. President Eisenhower desegregated the federal facilities in Washington, which flowed out to all federal facilities across the country. He is also credited with signing the first civil rights legislation since Reconstruction. The Civil Rights Act of 1957 provided new federal protection for voting rights and created a six-member civil rights commission with the right to investigate allegations of restricting voter rights. This act also established the civil rights division of the Justice Department.

It is not known whether anyone was investigated or prosecuted, and voting for black people went up only about 3 percent. The law was certainly needed in many Southern states. Orval Faubus's political career seemed to do a reversal when it came to civil rights. He ran for election in 1954 on promises of increasing school and road funding. After beginning his administration, he desegregated state buses and public transportation. From this, it appears that the governor was in favor of desegregation. This led to political attacks by Jim Johnson, a right-wing Democrat. These attacks and other influences caused Governor Faubus to reverse his political position on desegregation.

Unfortunately for Mr. Faubus, the crisis at Central High School destroyed his career. In politics, people have to be extremely careful when they choose sides. People who may appear supportive on certain issues could abandon the politician—leaving him or her with all the blame. Many politicians who stood with Governor Faubus on segregation campaigned against him on the same issue.

Even though Governor Faubus appeared to be against integration of schools in Arkansas, which meant he was against black people being allowed in certain places or positions, he won the 1962 election for governor with 81 percent of the black vote.

It wasn't that Mr. Faubus had the overall support of black people. Blacks in the South were strongly encouraged to vote when the results would benefit the candidate. It was more like an order.

History shows that many black people worked on farms in Arkansas. During the 1962 governor's election, the wealthy farmers who employed the workers paid their poll taxes. They were transported to the polls and told who to vote for. They were watched to make sure they did just as they were instructed. This was intimidation at the grandest scale. It was the very thing that Eisenhower's civil rights act was designed to prevent. The right to vote is not really a right unless people are allowed to make their own decisions.

Some presidents attempted to make civil rights better for black people in the past. President Harry S. Truman became president when Franklin D. Roosevelt died in office on April 12, 1945. Mr. Truman preceded President Eisenhower to the highest office in the land. Truman said he did not favor equality for black people, but he did want fairness and equality before the law.

Mr. Truman appeared to be a man of conviction when it came to the law, and he took his position seriously. He believed that the president had to rise above personal beliefs. When he developed convictions about the treatment of black people and their civil rights, he was determined to act—even if it meant political suicide. He signed Executive Order 9808 on December 5, 1946, which established a presidential committee on civil rights. He met and addressed the NAACP before he received a report from the new civil rights committee.

The committee's responsibility was to evaluate the state of civil rights in America, compile a report, and make recommendations to the president with respect to adoption or establishment. Mr. Truman's goal was to bring about change by legislation—or other means—to protect the civil rights of the people of the United States. The president also issued Executive Order 9980 to ensure equal treatment and hiring of black people for federal jobs. Executive Order 9981 integrated the military forces, but Executive Order 11051 revoked it in 1962.

When President Truman received the report from his civil rights committee, he was shocked. He felt that he could "no longer sit idly by and do nothing in the face of glaring injustice." He was convinced that the South was living eighty years in the past. The sooner they came out of it, the better it would be for them and the country. He was outraged by incidents of brutality on black citizens that went unpunished, especially when directed at black veterans. Isaac Woodard, a black sergeant, was dragged behind a bus in Batesburg, South Carolina. The police beat him until he was blinded.

The president's stomach was turned when black soldiers returning from fighting overseas were dumped out of army trucks in Mississippi and beaten. A friend of the president cautioned him to go easy on the civil rights issue. President Truman was going to try to remedy the situation even if he ended up not being reelected. He stated that failure would be for a good cause, but he was reelected with the help of the black vote.

Congress passed much civil rights legislation, throughout the years, but much of it was overturned. Some states paid no attention to following them, especially in the South. Nevertheless, President Truman held personal convictions against Negro injustice, and he was willing to take a stand for the things he believed in—without caving in to popular opinion. He allowed the presidency to overrule his personal upbringing and rose above his past bigotry. The country needs more men like him.

Franklin D. Roosevelt was elected as the thirty-second president to the United States on March 4, 1933. Some people think he did not do much in the area of civil rights. His plan was to follow the example or stance of previous presidents by not interfering with racial issues for black people. Nevertheless, the president did appoint a large number of black people to high positions.

In the middle of 1935, at least forty-five black people had positions in cabinet offices and New Deal agencies. They had a role in advising Mr. Truman on black employment, education, and civil rights issues, and the public began calling them "FDR's black cabinet." The president's wife was a great advocate for civil rights. Eleanor Roosevelt was photographed with civil rights leaders and was willing to fight for the cause. She often brought their issues to her husband—and sometimes received good results.

President Roosevelt's Executive Order 8802 declared, "There shall be no discrimination in the employment of workers in defense industries and in government, because of race, creed, color, or national origin." This was the first presidential directive on race since Reconstruction. It was thought by many, that President Roosevelt was influenced in this direction by his wife Eleanor, as well as Mr. A. Philip Randolph, who was president of the Brotherhood of Sleeping Car Porters. Mr. Randolph threatened to march on the White House lawn with up to fifty thousand black people, something that had never been done.

Eleanor Roosevelt was a vocal advocate of civil rights. Her support of the African-American cause made her unpopular among many whites in the South, but she was mostly responsible for the black support of the Democratic Party. She was a voice for black people in the White House, insisting that they receive more benefits from the New Deal programs created by her husband. She invited many black guests to the White House. She resigned from the Daughters of the American Revolution after they denied black singer Marian Anderson from singing in Washington's Constitutional Hall. She arranged for another concert on the steps of the Lincoln Memorial. Because of the spread of Aryanism, Eleanor Roosevelt was determined to fight even harder against American racism.

Mrs. Roosevelt was also a close friend of Walter White, the leader of the NAACP from 1931 to 1955. White and the First Lady—who also was a member of the NAACP from 1945 to 1962—had differences of opinions, but they honored and respected each other's opinions and views on civil rights. Eleanor Roosevelt tried to persuade her husband to sign legislation that would support black people and civil rights, but many of them fell short. She was a champion for black rights, and the black community respected her. After the death of her husband, Mrs. Roosevelt remained a focal point in American politics for another twenty years. She was bestowed the honor of First Lady to the World by President Harry Truman, and he appointed her as a delegate to the United Nations in 1946.

President Theodore Roosevelt became president in 1901 after the assassination of President William McKinley. Roosevelt was elected to his own term as president in 1904. Roosevelt is famous for many quotes, as well as being an author. Some of his quotes seem a bit outlandish, especially those concerning black people and Indians, but this was the norm for the time. His record would show that he worked to improve relations in civil rights. However, he did not get the support on civil rights issues that he sought for.

On October 16, 1901, Booker T. Washington—an educator, author, and orator—became the first black man invited to dinner in the White House by the president. Once the outcry and criticism from the white community began to be heard, the president caved to the pressure.

The president spoke out against racism and discrimination and appointed many black people to low-level federal offices. He was opposed to segregation and rejected anti-Semitism, but public outcry on issues the majority didn't support, such as desegregation, caused Roosevelt to change his public image.

On November 28, 1906, President Roosevelt ordered 160 black soldiers to be dishonorably discharged in Brownsville, Texas. The black men of the Twenty-Sixth Infantry Regiment of Fort Brown were not given hearings or trials. They were also denied back pay and pensions. There had been tension between the white soldiers in Brownsville and black infantrymen in nearby Fort Brown.

On August 14, 1906, rifle shots were fired. A white soldier was killed, and another one was wounded on a street in Brownsville. The white mayor and other white people in Brownsville made the assertion that it was done by the black infantrymen of Fort Brown. The white commanders at Fort Brown believed that all the black soldiers were in their barracks at the time and had nothing to do with the incident. The black soldiers also denied knowing or having anything to do with the incident.

President Roosevelt's dismissal of the black infantrymen caused great resentment among black people and criticism from some whites, but a Senate investigation upheld his decision in 1908. The army later conducted a new investigation in 1972 and reversed Roosevelt's order, but only one black soldier was still alive. Dorsie Willis was awarded a $25,000 pension on January 10, 1974—sixty-eight years after the injustice. It was the equivalent of $368 per year, and Mr. Willis died a year later.

Since Reconstruction, black people have fought to receive their constitutional rights. The law states that a person is considered innocent until proven guilty, but individuals with overwhelming evidence against them can plead not guilty and go free. Many black people feel that they have to overwhelmingly prove their innocence because they are presumed guilty until proven innocent. Statistics show that black men receive maximum sentences for their crimes while many of their white counterparts get off with a slap on the wrist.

History shows that many black people have not had equal or fair justice in the court system. Until the 1960s, black people were not allowed to sit on juries. Whites who were on trial for crimes against black people were pretty much guaranteed to get off.

In the twenty-first century, many black people struggle to receive their constitutional rights. Many other nationalities can come into America illegally and obtain the same rights without going through the proper avenues of obtaining citizenship. In other countries, people who violate laws while visiting might never get out of prison, but illegal aliens in America are allowed to vote, receive driver's license, and receive government benefits. They can receive all the rights of citizenship without being citizens. Only in America is this allowed to take place.

In the past, civil rights were mostly an issue for black and white people, where blacks fought to obtain the same rights as whites. On the fiftieth anniversary of the Civil Rights Act of 1963, Maria Shriver said, "So the civil rights issue is no longer a black and white issue; it's more like fifty shades of gray."

The civil rights issue has evolved to include many rights today, a great number of which will be discussed in the later chapters. One person's rights should not trample another person's rights as a citizen. Everyone should be judged equally and condemned equally. People coming into this country should be expected to accept the country as it is and become a part of it—loving it enough to stand up for it while embracing the liberty that it stands for. These ideas are not to be considered a fix for everything, but they are suggestions for where to start improving civil rights.

Dr. Martin Luther King Jr. probably said it best. His dream was "that one day America would live out the true meaning of its creed, that all men are created equal." He wanted all citizens to receive their equal rights. Rights are privileges that are reserved for the citizens of a country, state, or city.

For many years, black citizens were denied their constitutional rights because a certain segment of society felt that constitutional law did not apply to black citizens. Society considered them three-fifths human—even though the Constitution stated that all men were created equal in the sight of God. Black citizens—through their persistence and struggles—have finally obtained their rights.

Chapter 2

The Fight for Equal Rights in the Twenty-First Century

n the twenty-first century, many people are fighting for certain rights in the courts.

ENVIRONMENTAL RIGHTS

This movement was formerly known as the conservationist movement. The conservation movement has also been called the nature conservation and was involved in preserving natural habitats. The movement first concentrated on fish, wildlife, forestry, and plant life. As more people became involved, the federal government began to take steps toward preserving its national resources.

Congress passed its first conservation act in 1900. John Lacey was a member of the House of Representatives who was from Iowa. Mr. Lacy introduced a bill that President William McKinley signed into law on May 5, 1900. The Lacey Act made it a crime to transport illegally poached animals across state lines. On May 22, 2008, the Lacey Act was amended, expanding its protection to a broader range of plants and plant products.

When Leon Czolgosz assassinated President McKinley at the beginning his second term, Theodore Roosevelt became the twenty-sixth president. He was also the youngest president in the nation's history at the time. President Roosevelt was an avid outdoorsman who loved hunting and wildlife. Under his administration, great contributions were made to the conservation movement. He established the first federal wildlife refuge in Pelican Island, Florida. He also set aside more than 140 million acres for the national forest reserves. Mr. Roosevelt established the National Forest Service in 1905 and set up five new national parks. He also set aside eighteen additional sites as national monuments and instituted plans to preserve wildlife. With environmental issues, the environmental rights movement speaks out against almost all air pollution.

One of the largest environmental issues for the world is smog. Smog is fog mixed with smoke and chemical fumes. Even though smog is not as bad as it was in the early twentieth century, it still remains a problem in many cities. One of the most smog-infested cities in America in the twentieth century was Los Angeles. During World War II, residents of Los Angeles believed they were under a chemical attack by Japan because of the thick smog that covered the city. The smog caused stinging and burning in the eyes and caused people's noses to run. Visibility was no farther than three city blocks.

California would find out much later that the smog was the result of its own factories and motor vehicles.. The state went through many measures to find the cause. In the 1950s, Arie Haagen-Smit discovered that emissions from Californian's cars and factories were the major source of their problem. California was one of the major cities for automobiles and large factories. Mr. Smit discovered that ozone was the main source of the haze that hovered over the city. Not much was known about ozone at the time, especially as it related to pollution. The bluish, irritating gas has a pungent odor. This extremely reactive form of oxygen is a major air pollutant in the lower atmosphere, but it is a beneficial component of the upper atmosphere. Many scientists believe chemicals are depleting the beneficial part of the upper atmosphere.

Mr. Smit determined that smog was the cause of the bleach smell, eye irritation, and respiratory problems, but his report fell on deaf ears. Californians continued to build more expressways and factories, and things continued as they were. The smog was so bad on some days in California that children were kept home from school, businesses were encouraged to close, and the general public was asked to remain inside their homes. At times, children were kept inside, and large, smoke-producing factories were ordered to slow down their operations.

California made great changes to reduce its smog problems. In 1969, it issued emission-control standards and mandated that catalytic converters be installed on all automobiles. This resulted in catalytic converters being installed on all American cars. The ones on California vehicles had a special type of converter because of their serious smog problem. Other measures included vapor traps on fuel and solvent sources and soot screens on smoke stacks. California was not the only state with a smog problem, but it did seem to be the worst.

Donora, Pennsylvania had its own smog problem on Halloween weekend in 1948. A cloud hovered over the small town and remained there for five days. At least six thousand of the town's fourteen thousand residents became ill. The town depended on coal production, and the mills operated day and night. The coal heated the homes and powered the trains. The yellow grass in the town didn't seem to faze people as they went about their normal routines. Nobody thought the coal and zinc plants were causing a problem because the two industries provided the necessary jobs that fed the families and paid the bills. Even with the unusual cloud, activities in the town went on as usual.

People began to fall ill, experience shortness of breath and headaches, and vomit. The small hospital was overrun with patients, and the doctors worked overtime. By the time the course was run, twenty people had died, but the mills continued to operate as usual— without any consideration that they may have been the problem. Shutting down the coal and zinc mills of Donora would mean shutting down the economy of the town.

When the mill slowed its operations, people were able to breathe better. On Sunday morning, the front office of the local zinc mill shut it down for the day. On Monday morning, the smog lifted. A rainstorm washed away the smog and cleared the atmosphere. Donora was a prime example of air pollution harming citizens and wildlife.

Even though zinc has some health benefits, it only works in small doses. Exposure to large quantities can be fatal. Since the world's zinc production is increasing, more of it ends up in the atmosphere. Water can be polluted and poisoned by large quantities of minerals and chemicals that are dumped directly into the water as waste or absorbed into the atmosphere. When the chemicals are released into the air, they tend to mix with the moisture. Falling dew contaminates the ground and seeps into wells. Waste that is dumped into rivers has a tendency to contaminate fish, and the contamination is transferred to humans when the fish are consumed. These environmental issues affect the environment and the people who live in it.

In the town of Donora, the zinc and coal plants spewed large quantities of these contaminants into the atmosphere, the ground, and the water. Too many minerals actually hurt the environment and the residents. The major concern is determining how much waste can be released into the atmosphere or water without reaching dangerous levels.

In 1952, London experienced a "Killer Fog." The smog was so thick and toxic that buses could not run without guides with lanterns walking ahead of them. The cause appeared to be residents burning coal in their fireplaces and the large, coal-burning factories. When an extreme cold snap gripped the city, the cold air could not rise. With no air blowing to it away, the smog remained in the area. The "Killer Fog" took approximately twelve thousand lives. In 1956, British parliament passed a clean air act to clean up its environment and rectify its smog problem. The act outlawed the emission of dark smoke from chimneys and required companies to install new furnaces that would output smokeless emissions. These new furnaces also had to be fitted with chimneys that would keep grit and dust from emitting into the air. The factories had to change the type of fuel to power their plants.

The American government began to pass laws that would improve conditions in industrial cities and improve the environment. A clean air act that passed in 1963 began cleaning up air pollution and the environment. While the smog resolutions were not necessarily the result of the environmental movement, it was a major environmental issue that caused the country—and surrounding countries—to improve environmental conditions.

The largest environmental organization to date is Greenpeace, a nonprofit organization started in 1972 in Vancouver, Canada. It currently holds a membership of more than three million people and has registered offices in more than forty countries. Greenpeace has protested whaling, global warming, and nuclear testing. While these do not appear to be environmental issues, they are at the top of the environmentalist list. What appeared to be a good thing at the start of the conservation movement has become a protest against almost anything that the movement wishes to take on in the name of environmental rights.

Greenpeace has been known to speak out against logging, land management, overpopulation, depletion of natural resources, the fishing industry, and genetic engineering. The organization has campaigned against almost all forms of energy production besides wind and solar power, which make up approximately 2 percent of the world's energy supply. Reliance upon solar energy is increasing, and the American government is currently offering tax credits for citizens switching to solar energy.

As part of its vision statement, Greenpeace works to change government policies that it feels threaten the world's natural resources. Greenpeace feels that governments are not doing enough to protect the environment. In America we have the Environmental Protection Agency (EPA) which was established in 1970 to protect America's environment from pollution. Its job was to root out companies that polluted the environment and impose federal standards. Environmental issues are policed by the EPA, and they have been known to pose hefty fines on companies that contaminate the environment through chemical waste.

As with all movements, Greenpeace has its critics. Some people think Greenpeace is part of the environmental problem rather than the solution. Greenpeace is against cutting down trees, which is a large industry in America. Trees are used to build houses and building and selling houses grows our economy. Global warming, which is part of the Greenpeace agenda, is another issue. There are just as many scientists for it as there are against it.

Greenpeace has garnered problems through its protests on behalf of environmental issues. In 2013, the Russian coast guard arrested twenty-five Greenpeace activists as they attempted to hinder the work of a Gazprom oil rig in the Arctic Sea. The activists called themselves the Save the Artic Campaign and stated that energy exploration in the Arctic Sea posed a threat to the environment if there was an oil spill. The key word in that phrase was *if*.

Since 1970, the percentage of oil spills around the world has decreased from 246 to 33 spills in the year 2012 according to Our World in Data, which is supported by the Institute for New Economic Thinking. These oil spills have happened within 129 million square miles of the world's oceans. Given the amount of oil spillage compared to the vast amount of ocean and seas, that seems not nearly enough to shut down a company's operation. People must acknowledge the decrease in the number of oil spills over the decades as a willingness of companies to do a better job to prevent oil spills and not pollute the world's oceans. People should be able to see that rational people are concerned with waste and with pollution.

Greenpeace activists hung a sixty-foot banner outside the Procter & Gamble building in Cincinnati, accusing the company of causing danger to tigers. The organization was also known to cause irreparable damage to the Nazca site in Peru by posting a message next to a hummingbird geoglyph, ancient earth markings inscribed in the country's desert. There are many other examples where the world's largest environmental organization has seemed to overstep its bounds by protesting for environmental issues

Protest is a way of getting a message across, but the line has to be drawn when protest impedes progress by stopping production. Citizens are allowed to protest in the form of boycotts and marching. However, when it comes to slander, breaking and entering, and defacing personal and public property, the line has to be drawn. These actions are against the law. By doing these things, the movement becomes just as bad as those contaminating the environment.

The rights of the environment or the environmentalist should not supersede individual rights.

Greenpeace states as part of its belief, that if fossil fuels continue to be extracted, it will lead to climate change, which is currently a part of the environmental agenda. On the other hand the minerals that are stored in the earth are there for the people of the earth to use for living and surviving. Wherever there are minerals in the earth, humankind will find a way to extract them. They can be extracted more safely as better and cleaner ways are created on regular basis. If one mineral runs out, humankind will figure out how to mine another mineral for the world's continuation and survival.

ANIMAL RIGHTS

President Richard Nixon signed the Endangered Species Act in 1973 to protect animals that the public thought should be preserved. Under the Endangered Species Act, the federal government was given the responsibility to protect endangered species. It also addressed threatened species (those that are likely to become endangered in the near future) and critical habitats (those that are vital to the survival of an endangered or threatened species). The Game and Fish Commission makes recommendations and includes recommendations from the National Marine Fisheries Service. Outside groups and individuals are allowed to petition this federal organization for species that they think or feel are in danger. In some cases, the federal organizations have been bypassed altogether when people go directly to Congress.

The federal act helped preserve our national bird, the bald eagle, from extinction. In the early nineteenth century, many species were on the verge of extinction. Wild buffalos were slaughtered for their hides—and sometimes just for sport. In many cases, their carcasses were allowed to rot in open fields. Whales were hunted almost to extinction for blubber oil. Even though there was no established legislation at the time, concerned citizens worked to prevent the eradication of these great species. From their concerns, many of the rights movements formed.

The beliefs of these groups range from being against people wearing clothing made from animal skins, such as hats, coats, and purses, and eating meat. Models have been used in ads to promote the animal-rights agenda by posing nude. Even mass protests have been staged by naked people covered in blood to represent the killing and slaughtering of animals.

People for the Ethical Treatment of Animals (PETA) is the nation's largest animal rights organization and was founded in March of 1980. The group, led by Ingrid Newkirk, has more than three million members and supporters. PETA's mission statement says, "We also work on a variety of other issues, including the cruel killing of beavers, birds, and other 'pests' as well as cruelty to domesticated animals." Under the issues tab on their website, PETA says, "Animals are not ours to eat, wear, experiment on, use for entertainment, or abuse in any way."

PETA is against using animals for food and believes there are great health benefits to a vegan diet. While a vegan diet may be good, all of society should not be persecuted for eating meat or wearing clothing made from animal skins. If PETA is against using animals for food, it is their right not to eat meat—but they should not attempt to force all of society to follow their ideas because society also has rights. They should allow their ideas to be put in front of the general public and give the public the right to choose without fear of criticism. PETA also protests against family animal farms, which many people rely upon for a livelihood.

Even though these expressions are a part of PETA's doctrinal statement, PETA has been accused of killing animals through animal shelters in the United States. The organization that has been the most critical of PETA's practices is known as the Center for Consumer Freedom (CCF). The CCF's mission is to promote personal responsibility and protect consumer freedom. They believe that adult citizens should have the right to choose how to live their own lives and choose what to eat and drink.

The CCF publishes an annual review of the PETA organization, acting as its watchdog. The CCF accused PETA of killing 1,792 dogs and cats in 2013 in their Norfolk, Virginia, animal shelter. In their view, PETA practices a double standard, advocating animal rights on one hand while killing them through their animal shelters with the other.

PETA does state on its website that it euthanizes animals, but their defense is that the animals are unwanted, aggressive, sick, hurt, elderly, at death's door, or have no good homes available. The CCF stated, "A 2010 inspection of PETA's shelter by a veterinarian of the Virginia Department of Agriculture and Consumer Services discovered that 84 percent of the animals PETA took in were killed within twenty-four hours."

Will Coggin of CCF said that PETA might as well be called a "slaughterhouse." PETA is known to protest against slaughterhouses in its fight for animal rights. While the slaughter of animals for human consumption may look gruesome, it is a necessity to supply the world with meat needed for our human survival.The animal-rights movement and the environment movement appear to go hand in hand with the rights of animals. In their attempts to protect the environment, environmentalists fight for the survival of certain animal species, and the animal-rights movement wants to preserve all species. One would have to question whose rights should get precedence. Whose rights are more important—the animals or the human beings?

Animal-rights activists were protesting the use of guinea pigs, dogs, cats, monkeys, mice, and rats in scientific research long before the arrival of PETA. Animals have been an important part of medical research for many years, and it has played a great part in many medical advances, which has saved countless human lives. *World Book Encyclopedia* states, "The first known use of animals as medical research subjects was recorded by the Greek physician Galen in AD 100s."

One of the most well-known successful cases of animal research was the vaccination experiment of Louis Pasteur. Mr. Pasteur was a nineteenth-century scientist and chemist who made great strides in studying bacteria. He developed the process of vaccination, which helps the body fight off diseases. Because of Mr. Pasteur's studies, bacteria are better understood. Some strains can be deadly.

Pasteur wanted to apply the principle of vaccination to cure anthrax, which affected livestock, especially cattle and sheep. The disease was also thought to spread to humans. He prepared attenuated cultures of the bacteria after determining the conditions that led to the organism's loss of virulence. In the spring of 1881, Mr. Pasteur obtained financial support, mostly from animal farmers who had the most to lose or gain, to conduct a large-scale public experiment.

The experiment took place in Pouilly-le-Fort, on the southern outskirts of Paris. Pasteur immunized seventy farm animals, and the experiment was a complete success. The vaccination procedure involved two inoculations at intervals of twelve days with vaccines of different potencies. One vaccine, from a low-virulence culture, was given to half the sheep and was followed by a second vaccine from a more virulent culture than the first. Two weeks after these initial inoculations, both the vaccinated and control sheep were inoculated with a virulent strain of anthrax. Within a few days, all the control sheep died, but all the vaccinated animals survived. Because of Mr. Pasteur's successful experiment on the sheep, vaccination continues to be widely used today to prevent disease.

While some may be able to understand the protests and arguments of animal-rights activists against animal cruelty, animal research has played a very important part in the advancement of medicine in human society. The control sheep in Pasteur's experiment gave their lives for modern medicine, the survival of a very important food source, healing diseases, and providing a living for many farmers.

Some animal-rights activists argue against eating fish, but doctors continue to state that fish like salmon, which are rich in omega-3 fatty acids, are good for the health of human beings. Some animal-rights organizations view animals as persons and not property. With this mind-set, they are putting animals on the same level as human beings. In some cases, a person can get more jail time for abusing an animal than assaulting a person.

Animal-rights activists have protested with some success against what they feel are the extinction of certain species. Two of the most controversial species protected by activists are the spotted owl and the snail darter. Because of protests on behalf of the snail darter in

Tennessee, construction of a new dam was held up—and then halted after it was approximately 85 percent finished. The snail darter is a small fish that lives in shallow water. It looks like a minnow, but it is a member of the perch family. Biologists felt that the darter could not survive in deeper parts of the river because the dam would wipe out the shallow areas. Many isolated populations of snail darters were discovered in the Tennessee River after the building of the dam, and they were living in deep water.

The spotted owl was thought to be on the verge of distinction because of the timber industry. According to the *Christian Science Monitor*, "Spotted owls live in old-growth forest, that is, forest between 357 and 750 years old and dominated by huge Douglas fir and western hemlock trees." The federal government decided to set aside 9.5 million acres of land that it deemed critical for the survival of the spotted owl. Many animal-rights activists were still unhappy because they felt it was not enough.

The timber industry felt that the biggest threat to the spotted owl was the larger barred owl. Researchers agreed with the timber industry and began to kill off many of the barred owls. This procedure was stopped because of the cry of animal-rights activists. After many years of not cutting down old-growth trees, the spotted owl population continued to decline.

In these two instances, the animal-rights activists had it wrong. The dam in Tennessee did not destroy the snail darter, and the spotted owl population was not declining because of cutting down old-growth trees. In most cases, nature has taken care of itself when it comes to the survival of its species. One species may depend upon another for food, habitat, or survival, but in spite of the conditions, the species survive.

Different species adapt to new habitats as their environments change. Conservationists have studied these facts extensively. Even natural forest fires have been known to benefit the forest by getting rid of the underbrush, clearing the forest floor, and allowing sunlight to shine on new trees. For years, scientists have helped species survive and recover by moving them to more suitable habitats when their old habitats were destroyed.

Animal-rights activists may have some good ideas when it comes to preservation, but there has to be compromise on both sides. The logging industry cannot be expected to come to a complete halt because of an endangered species, and species shouldn't be wiped out for the sake of profit.

Even though some animal-rights organizations were started in other countries, America is a sounding board for activists around the world. While many of the environmental groups and animal-rights organizations have good ideas and causes, others seem a bit outlandish. There can be extreme sides to every issue. With the animal-rights groups, there are no compromises or happy mediums. It's as if their side is right and there are no other alternatives. Everyone has rights, and everyone's rights should be respected and acknowledged. They should not be taken away or disregarded. Human survival must take precedence over animal rights because human rights are the most important rights.

While the abuse of animals is wrong—and people should protect great species to preserve them for future generations to enjoy—they should not place animals above human beings. In the twenty-first century, the world has become full of people who love animals. Some people have been known to be extreme in their love for pets. Some households have as many as ten pets—even a mixture of dogs and cats. There was a time when dogs and cats were enemies, and dogs chased the cats. Now they are best friends without any rivalry.

Being an extreme animal lover is not a problem unless it becomes a nuisance to neighbors. When it comes to medical research, caution should be exercised instead of condemning all medical research on animals. People have to be cautious about excessive jail time for animal abuse. People should be punished or fined greatly, but they should not receive more time in jail for animal abuse than for human abuse.

Animal-rights movements that are against eating meat should be fought legally and challenged by society before the eating of meat is outlawed and everyone is forced to be a vegetarian. Because of the fear of animals being mistreated in movies, many producers have taken steps to make sure that animals are not abused during filming. They usually display a disclaimer to reassure the public.

LGBT RIGHTS

Members of the LGBT (lesbian, gay, bisexual, and transgender) community feel their sexual preferences should be considered a right in society. With the passage of recent legislation, they have obtained these preferences as rights. They consider it a right to be able to marry the same sex, adopt, and rear children. They have to go through the process of adoption because there is no way that two men or two women can reproduce.

The LGBT community is fighting for its rights and trying to make others accept its practices and lifestyles. Television screens are flashed in our faces with one show after another containing these practices, not to mention vulgar language. If an individual chooses to be a part of the LGBT community, that is his or her personal preference, but it's a problem when the attempt is pushed down the throats of others and people are forced to accept it or honor it as a right.

Society is beginning to embrace the idea of same-sex marriage, and with the recent Supreme Court ruling, it is now legal in all fifty states. A husband is a man, and a wife is a woman; according to God's law, a woman cannot be a husband any more than a man can be a wife. In the LGBT community, these are desires and preferences, but their personal sexual preferences and behaviors are now legal. They pushed it as normal behavior when it was abnormal behavior. In America, they have become successful, but in Africa and Russia, it continues to be against the law. While many Christian organizations are embracing this behavior, others continue to be against it. They want to keep marriage between a man and a woman, which was God's original design. These preferences certainly are not rights given by God, and they never will be, regardless of how many Christian churches are embracing it.

In the authorized King James Bible, Genesis states that God made male and female, blessed them, and instructed them to be fruitful and multiply. In it, the woman was the only suitable mate for the man. God said that it was not good for the man to be alone and made him a suitable helper. God made a woman and presented her to the man, and Adam was very pleased with God's presentation.

It takes male and female to procreate, and this is actually designed by God. Before God destroyed the world by flood—because corruption and violence filled the earth—he instructed Noah to take his wife, their three sons, and their wives into the ark. God instructed them to take two of every kind of animal species aboard (male and female). With this design of male and female, God chose to repopulate the earth. If the entire world goes in the direction of a man with a man and woman with a woman, there will cease to be repopulation. The human race will eventually die out. While fighting for rights of all kinds is prevalent in society, people should be more concerned about the survival of the human race.

When boys and girls reach puberty, they form an attraction to the opposite sex. If a boy or girl is feeling an attraction toward the same sex, this is an unnatural attraction and against nature. Nature teaches us this very natural concept, and people can see this behavior in the animal kingdom. It is not my intention to compare human beings to animals, but I am attempting to show the course of nature. In her book, entitled Dogs, Rebecca Stefoff explains the attraction between male and female dogs. The male dog pursues the female after she gives off her scent of being ready to mate. She does this by dividing up her urination into smaller portions while she is in estrus. Her body gives off hormones, which are chemical signals that the male dog can smell in her urine. This attracts the male dog to the female, serving as a sign that she is ready to mate, and he recognizes that she is in her season.

Nature teaches us lessons that if people follow and listen, they will do well. When people go against the course of nature, they go against the God-given design of the differences between the sexes. How do gay and lesbian couples decide who is going to be the husband and who is going to be the wife? In most lesbian and gay relationships, one of the women or men appears to be masculine, and the other appears feminine. There is a natural tendency to revert to masculine and feminine roles, which is natural according to the course of nature in relationships.

> For this cause God gave them up unto vile affections: for even their women did change the natural use into that which is against nature: And likewise also the men, leaving the natural use of the woman, burned in their lust one toward another; men with men working that which is unseemly, and receiving in themselves that recompense of their error which was meet. (Romans 1:26–27, KJV)

When women begin to lie with women and men begin choosing men instead, they are going against nature. This type of behavior is called sodomy, which is the practice of homosexual behavior as based on the laws of the Bible, and the people are referred to as sodomites. In 1 Kings 15:12, God caused King Asa to take away the sodomites out of the land, and removed all the idols that his father had made. If God does not accept this behavior as natural, why does the LGBT community feel this type of behavior should be accepted by society and be guaranteed rights under the Constitution? Prior to 1962, every state in the union had a law in some form or another against sodomy.

Gay and lesbian individuals often want to openly participate in certain activities or functions. Participating is not a problem because public functions are open to all individuals, and society don't discriminate because of sexual preference. The problem happens when gay and lesbian individuals want to use public functions as an opportunity to display their sexual preferences openly in the face of others—and force society to accept it as normal and natural.

In New York City, Mayor Bill de Blasio boycotted the 2014 Saint Patrick's Day parade because of tension with gay and lesbian groups. He said, "I simply disagree with the organizers of that parade in their exclusions of some individuals in the city" Mr. De Blasio won approval from the gay-rights community for boycotting the parade.

The parade organizers were not about completely excluding gay and lesbian individuals from marching in the parade, but they were against them marching openly like a protest demonstration. If a person wants to be gay, that is their prerogative and their choice to do so, but to push it as the natural way of life is completely against God and nature.

A similar incident happened in Boston, which has the second-largest Saint Patrick's Day parade in America. The Boston parade organizers invited Mass Equity to participate under the condition that its members not wear T-shirts or carry posters to identify their sexual orientation. Mass Equity decided not to march under those restrictions, stating it would be a return to the closet. The parade committee issued a press release since they didn't want to be perceived as bad guys by appearing as if they were totally against gay and lesbian rights. The parade organizers' intent was not to turn the traditional parade into a parade endorsing gay and lesbian rights. When such activity is allowed, it gives the impression that all are in agreement with gay rights. Some people feel that if the majority of authoritarians endorse it, then it must be acceptable.

Gays and lesbians were fighting for rights before 2010, but in October 2010, a federal judge issued an order to stop the controversial "don't ask, don't tell" policy of the military. President Bill Clinton instituted the policy on July 19, 1993. It was a compromise between those who wanted openly gay soldiers to be able to serve in the military. The law told the military not to ask individuals about their sexual preferences—and told individuals not to openly reveal it. The policy also restricted the US military from revealing closeted gay, bisexual, and lesbian service members, thereby allowing them to serve.

Judge Virginia A. Phillips of Southern California halted the policy in October 2010. Conservatives thought it was another case of liberal judges attempting to make policies that should only be done by Congress. Their stance was that democracy requires elected officials (not judges) to make social policy, but many federal judges appear to be insensitive to the consensus. Federal judges are overturning the will of the people on certain issues at alarming rates. The Senate overturned the "don't ask, don't tell" policy in December 2010.

"Coming out of the closet" became a popular phrase in the 1980s, and many gay and lesbian individuals openly declared their sexual preferences. At the same time, the HIV virus began to surface in the homosexual community. Many people died of the disease, and society began to look at HIV as a homosexual disease. Doctors have made great strides in the treatment of HIV and understand it better. It is no longer considered a homosexual disease.

Before the "don't ask, don't tell" law, the military could bar any openly gay individuals from entering the service. It didn't mean people couldn't be gay or lesbian and serve in the military. They had to keep it secret and not broadcast it publicly. The military said they were trying to protect high standards of morale. This military term deals with the mind-set of the troops or their emotional or mental conditions, especially in the face of opposition or hardship. This policy prevented gays or lesbians from disclosing their sexual orientations or speaking about their relationships. When gay people began to openly admit their sexual orientations, it appeared that they wanted the same from the military that they were receiving in society.

While the military was attempting to protect high standards and morale, high standards and morals were declining at an alarming rate in America and abroad. At times, it seemed to be vanishing. Morals deal with the principles of right and wrong in behavior. This decline of high standards and morals is creeping into American churches. Many churches are openly ordaining homosexuals to the ministry. It certainly seems that someone has missed the idea that the church gets its morals from the Word of God.

The large numbers of gay people coming out of the closet began to develop a voice and sympathy in society. This has led to many changes in the laws of society. Gay and lesbian individuals have protested for the right to marry and receive medical and spousal benefits. They are receiving these rights across the country.

The LGBT community wants sexual orientation to be considered a civil right—like race, color, and national origin. Many states have already added this preference to their discrimination policies. I certainly do not advocate discrimination in any form, but I believe that homosexuality is a choice of lifestyle and not a God-given right.

People can't help where they were born, the color of their skin, or their race, but they can choose their sexual preference? Should the personal preferences of the LGBT community be made into a constitutional right? Whose rights are right?

TRANSGENDER RIGHTS

Transgender or gender-identity rights are coming to the forefront in American society. It appears to be an offshoot of gay and lesbian rights. For the most part, individuals who claim to be transgender do not profess to be gay. They feel they are of the opposite sex. Even though they are male, they identify with the female gender and vice versa.

Many states are beginning to take up the issue of transgender rights in a serious way. It is described as a person's private or personal choice of gender identity. It doesn't matter what genitalia a person is born with, if a male feels that he is a female (or vice versa), he wants to be free to express it.

Some people say that the world is moving in the direction of no sexual differences, but there are sexual differences—and there always has been. No matter how some may not like the sex they are, they are what they are. However, with modern medical procedures, people are able to have sex-change operations, but a sex-change operation is not a fix. The problem is not in the genitals, but mental and emotional issues. It's their feelings that don't line up with the makeup of the body, and we all know feelings change like the wind. While a man may be able to have this procedure, he will never experience all the aspects of being a woman. Society has embraced, not only the transgender identity of Bruce Jenner, who now refers to himself as Caitlyn Jenner, but the transgender identity concept as a whole. It appears that anyone that does not agree with the transgender identity of individuals is considered by many as being out of the main stream.

According to former John Hopkins head psychiatrist Dr. Paul McHugh in an article he wrote in the Wall Street Journal, June 17, 2014.

> The transgendered suffer a disorder of "assumption" like those in other disorders familiar to psychiatrists. With the transgendered, the disordered assumption is that the individual differs from what seems given in nature—namely one's maleness or femaleness.

> This intensely felt sense of being transgendered constitutes a mental disorder in two respects. The first is that the idea of sex misalignment is simply mistaken – it does not correspond with physical reality. The second is that it can lead to grim psychological outcomes.

It appears that Dr. McHugh is saying the feeling of being transgender is all in the mind. This also points to the fact that the transgender states that they *identify* or *feel* they are of the opposite sex.

In Massachusetts, the commissioner of education, Mitchell Chester informed all his principals to allow boys and girls of any age who identify as transgender to use the public restroom and locker room of their choice. The commissioner's order came from a law that was passed in 2011; his hands were tied. House Bill 1589, presented by Byron Rushing and Carl Sciortino Jr., provided equal access to all public places, including hospitals, public transportation, nursing homes, supermarkets, and retail establishments. The proponents said the bill would stop discrimination in public accommodations, but there were already laws on the books against that type of discrimination.

In 2013, www.foxnews.com reported about a six-year-old transgender student in Colorado. The child, who was born a boy, identified as a girl. Since kindergarten, he had been allowed to use the girl's restroom. In December 2012, the principal said the child would have to use the boy's restroom or a gender-neutral one. The parents withdrew their son from the school and filed a complaint. The Transgender Legal Defense and Education Fund in New York filed a complaint on behalf of the child's parents, and they won the right for their son to use the girls' restroom. The mother of the boy stated that she only wanted the school to treat her son like the other little girls.

What does a six-year-old child know about gender identity? Children rely on their parents to teach them right and wrong, and this training has to start early. Some adults appear to be pointing children in the direction of being transgender—or they allow them to go in that direction without any guidance. They describe allowing individuals to choose which gender they want or feel as a personal choice. Society is going completely haywire when it begins to call a girl a boy or a boy a girl because that is what he or she feels they are. For rights, the wrong message is being projected. Issues like these confuse other children who are questioning, which is the truth.

Adults are supposed to protect and rear children to be responsible adults, guide and direct them the right way, and teach them to carry on the family heritage. In the twenty-first century people are choosing to teach children outrageous ideas. Young children do not know what they want; they have to be taught, trained, and instructed by parents. In many cases, when it comes to transgender issues or homosexuality, children are being severely misled.

If adults choose to be gay or lesbian, that is their prerogative. They have the privilege as long as it is not against the law. The catch-22 is that the people who push for this type of agenda have pushed it to become law so they will not be considered lawbreakers. It has to be understood that it may be allowed as a citizen's right, but it will not be accepted as a right given to us by God.

Restrooms in many public places already have unisex signs on them. They can be used by either sex—but not at the same time. These small, one-person restrooms are set up to accommodate either sex. When restrooms with more than one stall have to accommodate a larger number of people of the opposite sex at the same time, it can spell disaster. Common sense about rights appears to have gone out the window. The rights of all citizens have to be considered, addressed, and protected—not just the rights of a precious few.

In California, Governor Jerry Brown signed bill AB 1266 in 2013. It allowed boys and girls to choose whichever locker room they desired—regardless of gender. A boy who feels that he is a girl has a right to use the girls' locker room. The law also allows them to participate in the sports activity of their choice—even sex-segregated programs. The governor should not get all of the blame because the legislature passed the law first. The Senate passed the bill by a vote of 21–9, and the House passed it with a vote of 46–25. Politicians introduce outrageous bills that affect the public; legislators or senators may be opposed, but because of the sway of public opinion, they sit back and do nothing. Politicians run for office on certain platforms, and the people vote for them based upon their ideas. Once they are elected, some politicians forget about their constituents and espouse their own views. If legislators are absent when votes are cast on certain bills, they can say they did not vote for a bill when constituents cry foul. Being absent for a vote can be a vote in favor of a cause because one vote can defeat a measure.

In many cases, a minority is ruling the majority. Everyday working citizens with families do not have time to check every bill. They elect men and women to support and espouse their views and protect their rights.

However, there should be a limit to LGBT rights when expanding their rights will diminish the rights of others. This is already happening. Allowing gays and lesbians to marry will cause the continued breakdown and degeneration of society and the family unit. This is based upon common sense, which seems to go out the window with these issues. Years ago, there was much controversy among lawmakers concerning the absence of fathers in the home, which was causing the breakdown of families.

Now society is embracing two-women households or two-men households as if this will not create a problem in families. A real or complete family consists of male and female, as husband and wife as originally designed by God—not a male acting in the role of a female and vice versa. If this behavior were correct or acceptable by God, the twin cities of Sodom and Gomorrah would not have been destroyed. When society is pushed to accept abnormal behavior or conduct as normal, society will begin to degenerate and start on a course of destruction. In such cases, people don't realize their mistakes until they see the devastation many years later.

CHRISTIAN RIGHTS

Christian rights are under attack in the twenty-first century, and the attacks are on the rise. The First Amendment guarantees the freedom of religion to every American citizen. This freedom is under attack in Christian institutions, churches, marriage, the military, children, and the public arena. Society seems to be making it a major offense to be a Christian in America, even though America is founded upon Judeo-Christian principles. Christian rights are currently protected under the Constitution. The rights under attack include Christian prayer, the biblical concept of marriage, Christian beliefs, and the display of anything that promotes God.

There is a constant fight against Christian prayer and the Pledge of Allegiance because of the "one nation under God" sentence. Congress has always opened its sessions with prayer, but on November 6, 2013, the Supreme Court took up a case to consider whether prayer should still be allowed in government meetings.

Two women from Greece, New York, brought the complaint. One woman was Jewish, and the other was an atheist. They felt they were being left out of town hall meetings because Christians were always leading the prayers. The town board had been opening its sessions with Christian prayers since 1999. On May 5, 2014, a ruling came down in favor of the town. The Supreme Court decided in a 5–4 ruling that legislative bodies such as city councils are within their rights to begin their meetings with prayer—even if it plainly favors a specific religion. The Supreme Court further ruled that Christian prayer before government meetings did not violate the constitutional prohibition against government establishment of religion; the justices cited history and tradition.

Justice Anthony M. Kennedy wrote for the court's conservative majority:

Ceremonial prayer is but a recognition that, since this nation was founded and until the present day, many Americans deem that their own existence must be understood by precepts far beyond the authority of government.

That was not the first time the issue of Christian prayer has come before the Supreme Court. In 1983, the court ruled that the Nebraska legislature did not violate the Constitution by opening its sessions with prayer. The court upheld the practice in a 6–3 decision. Chief Justice Warren Burger issued the opinion for the court. Justice Burger rested the court's opinion on the historical custom that prayers by tax-supported legislative chaplains could be traced to the First Continental Congress and the Bill of Rights. He said the practice had become "part of the fabric of our society." The invocation for divine guidance was not an establishment of religion. "It is simply a tolerable acknowledgment of beliefs widely held among the people of this country." People should be able to see that the Constitution of the United States supports Christianity—at least in the form of Christian prayer as a right.

Concerning the issue of traditional biblical marriage, most devout Christians believe in—and also stand against same-sex marriages. In many cities and states, Christianity is being attacked because of its belief that marriage should be between one man and one woman. Christians view the Bible as the truth from God.

An Oregon man closed his bakery because of attacks from gay-rights activists after a customer tried to purchase a wedding cake. The baker asked the customer the names of the bride and groom for the cake, and the young woman said there were two brides. The owner of the bakery said he could not do the cake based on his religious principles. After leaving the bakery, the customer filed a complaint. The owner of the bakery stated that he did not refuse to serve homosexuals, and that his store was frequently visited and patronized by homosexuals. His religious principles would not allow him to make a cake for a same-sex marriage.

Due to protests, signs, and vicious phone calls and e-mails from gay rights activists, the baker decided to shut the doors of the shop and move his business back to his home. The baker apparently felt that he had every right to exercise his convictions and base his business on his religious freedom. Lesbian couples say they have every right to have a wedding cake made by the bakery of their choice. Whose right is right?

Society fails to understand that the Christian baker making the cake the way the customer wanted would have been an endorsement of the idea of the lesbian wedding. This is where religious convictions come in to play. Christians are bound by principles to treat everyone right and fairly, but they are also bound by their convictions not to endorse behavior that even God does not endorse. To do so would be a slap in the face of God and his Word, which the Christian is expected to obey. To embrace something that God hates would be to go against God.

While God loves all human beings, he certainly does not love or agree with sinful behavior. God sent his Son into the world to die for the sins of all humankind, so that humankind would not have to continue in sin, but forsake it, believing and embracing Jesus Christ as the Savior. Christ came into this world to save people from their sins—not to endorse those sins. The Savior did not come into the world to condemn us because he knew that people were already under condemnation. He made a way so people would not have to continue in sin. Christians serve a loving God.

Society needs to understand that Christian principles are Godly principles; the ideas cannot be separated. God delivered his laws to the Hebrew people. He chose them out of all the races to be the avenue to introduce himself and his standards to the human race. God brought his son into the world through this race of people.

In God's law, as written in the book of Leviticus 18:22, it is stated that man shall not lay with mankind as he would womankind, for such is an abomination to God. There are more examples listed in the Bible that confirm God's hatred for this type of activity besides the story of Sodom and Gomorrah. To put it plainly, God is against men having sex with men and women having sex with women. As previously stated, it goes against the course or laws of nature. If God does not endorse the behavior of homosexuality, he will certainly not sanction the marriage. A large segment of society is endorsing this behavior while condemning Christians for not endorsing it.

Many devout Christians believe that marriage is honored by God when done according to God's standards as written in the King James Version Bible. A minority believes marriage should also be between two women or two men, but it is quickly increasing.

Some have even taken it further in marrying their pets or self-portraits. The list gets stranger by the day and by the year, yet there is seemingly no outcry against it. When people speak out against things like these that are immoral by any standard, they will be attacked as though they are the ones who are wrong—and then the outcry is against them.

The Christian standard was laid out in the Declaration of Independence. Like the preamble to the Constitution, it mentions the laws of nature and the nature of God. It spells out the beliefs of the Founding Fathers as they began to form a more perfect union. It states that people are given rights by God that cannot be taken away. From these great documents, people see that God is respected and honored in the formation of this great nation. Are people expected to abandon these standards and Christian beliefs so that no one in society will be offended?

Anyone can be a Christian in name, but the Word of God expects Christians to be Christian in practice. When people convert to Christianity, they are expected to embrace Christian principles by adopting the lifestyle that Christianity demands. Not all people who call themselves Christians in name are Christians in practice. This is evident when Christians endorse homosexual lifestyles. God has only one law book for all Christians. There is not a separate Bible or set of scriptures for Christians who embrace homosexual behavior.

> Whosoever transgresses and abides not in the doctrine of Christ has not God. He that abides in the doctrine of Christ, he has both the Father and the Son. (2 John 1:9)

John goes on to say that if someone does not embrace this teaching, Christians should not receive them into their houses or offer them prosperous journeys. That is why Christians do not embrace the homosexual way of life.

When people wear Christian names but do not live Christian lives, it has the tendency to reflect upon all Christians. Christianity has to be lived and practiced to be real Christianity. In today's society, Christians are being asked to give up their rights so that others will not be offended. Christian rights are under attack from the outside and from within by the very ones who say they embrace the teachings of the Bible.

In 2014, a preacher in Dallas vowed to perform gay weddings regardless of the consequences from the United Methodist Church. The UMC doctrinal statement said, "The church affirms the sanctity of the marriage covenant and shared fidelity between a man and a woman. We support laws in civil society that define marriage as the union of one man and one woman." However, some UMC pastors decided to go against church doctrine and perform the ceremonies regardless to what the Word of God says about that lifestyle. How can you embrace Christianity without embracing every word of the Bible?

There appear to be no signs of Christian convictions when pastors are going against every Christian belief that the Bible speaks of. Such people might as well throw away the Bible and write their own because it appears that's what's happening.

Another Methodist preacher in Dallas, who had been pastoring for forty years, reported that he had a large number of gay and lesbian members in his flock. He vowed to perform gay and lesbian weddings regardless of the consequences. Maybe no one told him that the purpose of church is to save sinners, and sinners are not saved until they are converted and learn not to practice sin. There seems to be an attempt to erase the word *convert* from the Christian language, but it is a vital part of the Christian faith. Jesus Christ instructed Peter to strengthen his brothers in the faith after he converted. John the Baptist's message about repentance was a message of conversion. He told people to repent and do works that were pleasing to God. The whole concept of the Christian faith is to please God.

A Methodist pastor in Lebanon, Pennsylvania, stated that he performed his son's gay marriage in good conscience. However, he went against church law by performing the marriage. In the Bible, that is heresy, and the pastor would be considered a heretic. The minister said he took God's love and extended it to his son. Love for humankind does not endorse love of sinful practices. Christians extend God's love to people by loving them regardless of their chosen lifestyle, but they also tell them the truth, which is that God does not accept such behavior. People are instructed to come as they are, but when a person embraces the Christian faith, the Bible says, "Be ye transformed."

To extend God's love to people, Christians must share the love of God and tell people the truth about what God desires. We should not mislead people into thinking God will accept behavior that God has said he is against. Love people enough to tell them that God loves them, but God also wants them to change and help them do so.

When it comes to God, that preacher had it backward. Jesus Christ, who speaks for God, made the statement that we have to love God more than our family members and our own selves or we cannot be his disciples. He further stated that if we loved our parents and siblings more than him, we are not worthy of him. Christians do not violate the Word of God to please people and make them feel accepted in their chosen lifestyles—no matter how much they love their family and friends. This seems to be a harsh statement, but with proper understanding, it is not harsh at all. Christians have to value an eternal heavenly life with God more than a measure of life on earth with loved ones.

The pastor went on trial in the church for violating the church law, but he continued to hold his license on appeal. God's Word is certain on homosexual behavior, the proper concept of marriage, and the Christian stance on such issues. God's Word is settled in heaven, and Christians cannot change it. It is written that Christians should not add too or take away from the Word of God.

Revelations 22:18-19 For I testify unto every man that hears the words of the prophecy of this book, If any man shall add unto these things, God shall add unto him the plagues that are written in this book. And if any man shall take away from the words of the book of this prophecy, God shall take away his part out of the book of life, and out of the holy city, and from the things which are written in this book.

If Christians add to it, they add to the plaques mentioned, which will come upon lives. If Christians take away from the words written, they take their parts out of it. In other words, they lose their inheritance of eternal life.

Most Christians are not attempting to push their religion upon others. They just want the opportunity to practice it and live it freely based upon their Christian convictions.

Christianity in America has been under an attack, but citizens have supported legislation in an attempt to ensure their Christian rights. In Arizona, Governor Jan Brewer vetoed a bill in 2014 that she felt would have created more problems than it was intended to solve. The bill was based upon a Colorado bakery that a judge ordered to cater a same-sex wedding. The bill would have allowed Christian businesses to deny service to gay and lesbian customers, thereby discriminating against them. Because of these fears, recent laws have included sexual orientation as part of the discrimination process that included not discriminating against people for their sex, race, or marital status.

The rights issues in America and around the world are becoming more complex. Where it will end up is anybody's guess. While the Arizona bill may not have been a good bill, and the governor of Arizona may have been right, we have to consider the reasons behind the introduction of the bill. In court systems around America, Christians are being told that they have to provide the service that the customer wants regardless to whether or not it violates their religious convictions or offends them. The intent of the bill was to protect Christian rights.

According to Religious hostility.org, which is a report distributed by the Family Research Council of Washington, DC, a list of attacks has been made on the Christian faith. This organization reports on all violations of religious freedom. This chapter focuses on the Christian ones.

A Christian counselor for the Center for Disease Control (CDC), Marcia Walden, was fired because she refused to lie about why she was referring clients with same-sex relationship problems to other counselors. Walden told a homosexual client that her personal values would interfere with the client-therapist relationship and never mentioned her religious objections. In response, the client complained to the CDC that Walden was homophobic. Walden reiterated to her supervisors that she had no problem counseling homosexual individuals, but her religious beliefs prevented her from conducting relationship counseling for those in homosexual relationships. Her supervisors suggested that she lie to homosexual clients and tell them she did not have much experience with relationship counseling. Walden refused to lie about why she was referring clients, and she was ultimately fired for not "altering her approach." The Eleventh Circuit rejected claims that Walden's rights were violated under the First Amendment, affirming the district court's summary judgment ruling against her.

When Marcia Walden would not violate her Christian beliefs by counseling the same-sex couple, she was encouraged to violate her beliefs by lying to them, and when she refused to do so, she was fired. If Ms. Walden had counseled the same-sex couple with their marital problems, she would have been forced by her convictions to tell them that the source of their problem was the marriage itself. This was the reason she referred them to someone else. If she had counseled them according to her convictions, she would have jeopardized her employment. As it turns out, she was fired anyway. Where was her right to her belief?

In 2012, Prudhomme's Lost Cajun Kitchen, a Pennsylvania-based restaurant, was offering discounts to individuals who brought in a church bulletin on Sundays. After complaints, the restaurant was forced to give the discount to anyone with a bulletin from any congregation, including atheist ones.

School officials in the Brawley Union School District threatened to mute Brooks Hamby's microphone if he mentioned God is his graduation speech.

Every year, Twin Cities Pride, a LGBT advocacy group, hosts a gay pride festival in a public park in downtown Minneapolis. Subject to city approval, vendors of all kinds are allowed to set up booths in order to sell their wares to the public. However, when Brian Johnson, an evangelical Christian, requested a booth to distribute Bibles, the city denied his application and proceeded to pass an ordinance that limited the distribution of materials in booths and throughout the park. Johnson filed a lawsuit to request an injunction against the discriminatory regulation. In a 2–1 decision, the US Court of Appeals for the Eighth Circuit reversed the district court's original denial of Johnson's request.

These are just a few examples where Christians' rights were denied or violated, and in many cases, the court system ruled against the Christians. The fight against believing in God for Christians is becoming a major crime in America. If people mention the name of Jesus, they may be crucified, *so to speak.*

Many people consider displays of Christianity offensive, but Christians are expected to accept deviant behavior in society because society has the right to do it. People can make any kind of public display in society, but there will be a major uproar about any Christian displays.

A Satanist group was advocating the placement of a satanic statue at the state capitol in Oklahoma City. The statue would be Satan embracing two children and was designed so people could sit in his lap. It came about after a monument to the Ten Commandments was placed on the capitol lawn as a gift from State Representative Mike Ritze.

Lucien Greaves, the spokesman for the Satanic Temple, said the statue is designed to reflect the views of Satanists. The ACLU filed a lawsuit against the original monument, but the matter was not resolved. Eventually the statue was placed in a satanic Temple in Detroit, Michigan. About 700 people gathered at the temple on July, 25, 2015 to unveil the 9 –foot monument to Baphomet, which is a symbol of Satanism. There is a constitutional right for the commandments to be displayed since Christianity has some support from the Constitution. America's laws are based upon the commandments God gave to Moses to spread throughout the world.

America has to go back to its pledge to be "one nation under God with justice and liberty for all." America appears to have forsaken the moral laws of God and replaced them with their own laws, which are laws that suit and fit themselves. Just like the presidents of Babylon in the days of Daniel the prophet, we are quickly beginning to outlaw the things of God. Laws are being passed—and enforced—that outlaw the display of religious symbols in workplaces.

Christian rights should not be taken away because non-Christians are offended. Christians are not attempting to take away rights from others. They are fighting for the right not to be forced to endorse the rights of people who go against their core Christian beliefs. The Constitution states that Congress shall make no law respecting the establishment of a religion or prohibiting the free exercise of religion, but we are headed toward busting the First Amendment to pieces by prohibiting the free exercise of Christianity. Anything else appears to be acceptable. Christian businesses should not be forced to provide birth control, contraceptive coverage, or abortion coverage in their insurance plans—or to go against their religious beliefs. Whose right is right?

Chapter 3

Abortion Rights

Abortion rights in America began with the passing of the Supreme Court ruling entitled Roe v. Wade in 1973. In Dallas, Norma McCorvey was denied an abortion. Her legal pseudonym was Jane Roe, and she filed a suit against Henry Wade, the district attorney of Dallas County. When the Texas court ruled that the law against abortion was unconstitutional, Mr. Wade appealed to the Supreme Court, and the rest is history.

Before the court decision, approximately thirty-one states had antiabortion laws. Now it is legal in every state in the union. Even though Norma McCorvey's case brought the abortion issue before the Supreme Court, she never received an abortion. She was a waitress and felt that receiving an abortion should not be against the law. She later converted to Christianity and eventually became an advocate against abortion.

The Supreme Court adopted the view that the fetus was not a living person and was not entitled to constitutional protection. The ruling only allowed abortions within the first trimester; states were expected to regulate it during the second trimester. Abortions could only be done in the third trimester if the life of the mother was at stake. Some abortions have been done in the third trimester even though the mother's life was not at stake.

Abortions were outlawed in public hospitals and clinics, and public employees were prohibited from assisting in the procedures. With abortion rights, there are two well-known viewpoints: pro-life and pro-choice. The pro-life activists believe that abortion is wrong because the fetus is considered alive at conception, and they are against abortion for any reason. The pro-choice activists believe it should be up to the mother to choose because it is her body and abortion is a private matter. This is the argument that was taken before the Supreme Court. The court based its decision upon the Fourteenth Amendment, stating that the Texas law violated a woman's right to privacy.

After the court ruling, Medicaid paid for many procedures, but the Supreme Court changed it 1977. The case was won on the idea of a woman's privacy being violated, yet public tax dollars were used to help her receive an abortion. This seemed to be a case where individuals argue for the right to do as they please and expect the government to pay for it with taxpayer dollars. Opponents of abortion have stated that it is a woman's right to choose—and the government should not be involved—but the funding causes the government to be involved. People are very much in favor and willing to take government money to take care of their private matters.

Before 1976, Medicaid funded approximately 300,000 abortions annually. In 1976, Representative Henry Hyde, a Republican from Illinois, introduced an amendment to limit federal funding of abortion that later passed through the legislature. After the Hyde Amendment went into effect in 1977, federally funded abortions began to decrease annually, dropping to 182,000 that year. In 1986, the number dropped to 232, and it dropped to 109 in 2000. With the decline in the number of abortions, it appears that the majority of women only wanted them if the government was paying for them.

After the passing of the Affordable Care Act, it appears that Planned Parenthood, which is the nation's largest abortion provider, will get $655,000 in federal funds in the form of grants for abortions. Planned Parenthood in Iowa is expected to receive $214,427. The Intermountain Planned Parenthood Inc. of Montana will receive $295,604, and Planned Parenthood of Northern New England, in New Hampshire, will receive $145,161. With this funding to the Planned Parenthood organization, it appears that government funding for abortion is now back in the game. Planned Parenthood is thought to be the largest provider of abortions in America.

The Affordable Care Act, which has been labeled as Obamacare, was passed in the Senate on December 24, 2009, and in the House of Representatives on March 21, 2010. President Obama signed it into law on March 23, 2010, and the Supreme Court upheld it on June 28, 2012. The health-care law has attracted major opposition and legal challenges from religious and conservative groups for requiring insurers to cover the cost of birth control. In 2015, the Supreme Court continued to scrutinize Obamacare but upheld it in a 6-3 vote.

With abortion rights, it seems as though someone else's rights are violated: the unborn child. The unborn child or fetus is not able to speak for itself. It needs advocates to speak on its behalf—just as newborns and toddlers need representatives. Whose rights are right when it comes to abortion—the mother's or the fetus?

Another important thing to consider when speaking about abortion is that fathers are almost never mentioned. It requires one in order for a woman to get pregnant. What about his rights?

Abortion involves the death of a fetus while still in the mother's womb. The method of abortion depends upon the stage of pregnancy and the size of the fetus. The technical definition is a pregnancy that is terminated before birth. Since the passing of Roe v. Wade, there have been many types of abortion methods used. The most common methods are mifepristone and misoprostol, suction aspiration, dilation and evacuation, and late-term abortions.

MIFEPRISTONE AND MISOPROSTOL (RU-486)

RU-486 is also known as the abortion pill. It is the most popular method used in early pregnancies. While the amount of traditional abortions is on the decline, use of the abortion pill is on the rise. Statistics state that abortion via RU-486 is up approximately 22 percent per year, accounting for 14 percent of total abortions.

French scientist Etienne Emile Baulieu created and designed RU-486 in 1970, and other countries approved it in 1988. It hit the United States in September 2000. The pill can be used to end pregnancy at up to nine weeks. The first step is ingesting a dose of mifepristone tablets by mouth, which causes the placenta to separate from the endometrium. It also softens the cervix and increases contractions. The second dosage of tablets, which is known as misoprostol, is ingested within forty-eight hours of the mifepristone. The misoprostol causes uterine contractions to make the body pass the uterine contents like a miscarriage.

The pills are not a total fix in every occasion and can cause severe cramping, nausea, dizziness, shivering, chills, hot flashes, headaches, diarrhea, vomiting, and vaginal bleeding. In some cases, the medication may not end the pregnancy; in that case, traditional suction-type abortion must be used.

SUCTION ASPIRATION

Suction aspiration, which is also known as vacuum aspiration, is commonly used and consists of two methods: manual vacuum and machine vacuum.

Manual vacuum is a procedure that can be used during the first trimester. This procedure uses a specially designed syringe to apply suction and remove the contents of the uterus. In the twelfth week of pregnancy, the fetus is less than two inches in length.

The machine vacuum procedure uses a hollow tube that is attached to a bottle and an electric pump that provides a vacuum. The vacuum is 27–29 times more powerful than a normal household vacuum. The woman may feel some pain during or after this procedure, but if all goes well, the patient may resume normal activities the next day.

DILATION AND EVACUATION

This procedure is performed from twelve weeks to the twenty-sixth week of pregnancy (the second trimester). The uterus is scraped with a sharp spoon-like instrument. The fetus and the placenta are extracted with forceps that are inserted into the womb to pull apart the fetus. This process is repeated until the entire fetus is dismembered. Premature labor may be induced by using prostaglandin to soften the cervix. Does the fetus have rights? In some cases, it does, but in other cases, it doesn't.

The fetus does not have rights until a certain number of weeks, but when a pregnant woman is murdered, the individual is charged with two murders. How is the individual charged with the murder of something that is not considered to be alive in the first place? That was the Supreme Court's decision in 1973.

The Supreme Court did not consider the fetus a living person. In many cases across the country, people have been charged with the death of a fetus. In Modesto, California, Scott Peterson murdered his wife and her unborn child or fetus. Laci Peterson was eight months pregnant with Conner at the time of her death. A new law outlaws fetal homicide (feticide). There is a contradiction in how the laws have been interpreted when it comes to abortion, the definition of a fetus, and determining when life begins.

LATE-TERM ABORTION

Late-term abortions are also known as partial-birth abortion. President George W. Bush signed legislation in 2003 that made performing a partial-birth abortion a federal crime. The law made it illegal for a doctor to partially remove an intact fetus from a woman's body before aborting it, usually by crushing its skull. The law did not mention a gestation period or number of weeks of pregnancy—only the procedure used.

> The Congress finds and declares the following: A moral, medical, and ethical consensus exists that the practice of performing a partial-birth abortion— an abortion in which a physician deliberately and intentionally vaginally delivers a living, unborn child's body until either the entire baby's head is outside the body of the mother, or any part of the baby's trunk past the navel is outside the body of the mother and only the head remains inside the womb, for the purpose of performing an overt act (usually

the puncturing of the back of the child's skull and removing the baby's brains) that the person knows will kill the partially delivered infant, performs this act, and then completes delivery of the dead infant—is a gruesome and inhumane procedure that is never medically necessary and should be prohibited.

Why did it take seventy-eight years to come to the understanding that abortion in the third trimester is gruesome and inhumane? Should we stay on the course we started on when the Supreme Court outlawed partial-birth abortion? That brought common sense to the idea of abortion. Since the law states that a fetus cannot be aborted in the third trimester, it should be evident that a fetus has rights like another person. If a fetus is not considered a living being and has no rights, why do we have laws to protect the unborn? How can a person be charged with murdering something that is not alive?

Partial-birth abortion has been banned, and Supreme Court has ruled that it is unconstitutional. Somebody has gotten the point across that late-term abortions were actually killing babies. It's hard to figure how anyone could have come to any other conclusion if they've read the procedure that doctor's use in such abortions. The fight for unborn children should continue until abortion is against the law again. If a woman does not want a child, she should refrain from the behavior that brings children into the world: having unprotected sex.

In 2013, a Philadelphia doctor was found guilty of murdering infants and involuntary manslaughter in the drug-overdose death of a patient who had undergone an abortion in his clinic. Dr. Kermit Gosnell had been performing late-term abortions in his clinic since 1979. Dr. Gosnell has been breaking the law since 2003. The jury in Mr. Gosnell's trial was informed that he kept at least forty-seven babies in odd places at his clinic, including cat food jars and other containers. Dr. Gosnell was sentenced to life in prison without parole after waiving his right to seek an appeal in exchange for the state not seeking the death penalty.

There are cases around the world that involve aborted fetuses being found in dumpsters or being burned to power homes in Oregon. Two doctors were charged with murder in Elkton, Maryland, after three dozen frozen fetuses from twenty to thirty-five weeks old were found in a freezer in their clinic. Neither doctor lived in Maryland, but they allegedly operated a clinic in the area. Neither doctor was convicted.

Whose right is right—the woman or the child? What about the rights of the sperm donor? No one ever mentions the man when it comes to aborting a child. The woman could not have gotten pregnant by herself. Whose right is right?

BLACK GENOCIDE RIGHTS (THE NEGRO PROJECT)

Margaret Sanger, founder of Planned Parenthood, developed the Negro Project as a eugenic plan for black Americans. Ms. Sanger promoted the idea of eugenics, which is a science that tries to improve the human race by controlling which people become parents. It is further defined as a science that attempts to improve society by controlling human mating of hereditary qualities of a race. This eugenic plan of Margaret Sanger and her followers was accomplished through the process of abortion and other means. This black genocide focused mainly on aborting black babies, controlling and limiting the growth of the black population.

Margaret Sanger was born Margaret Higgins on September 14, 1879, in Corning, New York, to Michael Hennessy Higgins and Anne Purcell Higgins. As one of eleven children born into a Roman Catholic Irish-American family, her ideals were formed early. She thought the early death of her mother was due to her mother's many pregnancies. She was deeply troubled by what she felt contributed to her mother's demise and determined that she would not have the same fate.

Margaret received support from her two older sisters while attending Claverack College and Hudson River Institute before enrolling in White Plains Hospital as a nurse probationer in 1900. As a practical nurse in the women's ward, she was working toward her registered nursing degree when she married architect William

Sanger in 1902. Her marriage to Mr. Sanger ended her formal nursing training, and she began to have children.

Margaret began to get seriously involved in radical politics and started a publication promoting a woman's right to birth control. Sanger started her campaign to educate women about sex in 1912 by writing a newspaper column called "What Every Girl Should Know." She also worked as a nurse on the Lower East Side of Manhattan, which was a predominantly poor immigrant neighborhood.

Through her work, Mrs. Sanger treated a number of women who had undergone back-alley abortions or tried to self-terminate their pregnancies. She objected to what she felt was the unnecessary suffering of these women, and she fought to make information about birth control and contraceptives available. She also began dreaming of a "magic pill" that could be used to control pregnancy. Sanger said, "No woman can call herself free until she can choose consciously whether she will or will not be a mother."

In 1914, Sanger started a feminist publication. *The Woman Rebel* promoting a woman's right to birth control. The monthly magazine landed her in trouble since it was illegal at the time to send information on contraception through the mail. The Comstock Act of 1873 prohibited the trade and circulation of "obscene and immoral materials."

Anthony Comstock championed the law and included publications, devices, and medications related to contraception and abortion in his definition of obscene materials. It also criminalized mailing and importing anything related to these topics.

Rather than face a possible five-year jail sentence, Mrs. Sanger fled to England. While there, she worked in the women's movement and researched other forms of birth control, including diaphragms, which she later smuggled back into the United States.

By that time, she had separated from her husband, and the two later divorced. Margaret Sanger was known to embrace the Malthus theory, which promoted the concept of eugenics. Ms. Sanger then aligned herself with the eugenicists whose ideology prevailed in the early twentieth century. Eugenicists at the time strongly espoused racial supremacy and purity, particularly of the Aryan race. Eugenicists hoped to purify the bloodlines and improve the race by encouraging the fit, as they called them, to reproduce and the unfit "in their minds" to restrict their reproduction. They sought to contain the inferior races through segregation, sterilization, birth control, and abortion.

Thomas Robert Malthus was a nineteenth-century cleric and professor of political economy. He believed the human population was like a time bomb that threatened the existence of the human race. He viewed social problems such as poverty, deprivation, and hunger as evidence of his theory.

George Grant stated that Malthus condemned charities and other forms of benevolence because he believed they only exacerbated problems. Malthus wanted to restrict population growth within certain groups of people. Malthus theories of population growth and economic stability became the basis for national and international social policy during that time.

Thomas Malthus published an essay on the principle of population. He published six editions of "Magnum Opus" under an assumed name between 1798 and 1826. In the essay, he said, "All children born, beyond what would be required to keep up the population to a desired level, must necessarily perish, unless room is made for them by the deaths of grown persons. We should facilitate, instead of foolishly and vainly endeavoring to impede, the operations of nature in producing this mortality."

His followers believed that in order for Western civilization to survive, the physically unfit, the materially poor, the spiritually diseased, the racially inferior, and the mentally incompetent had to be suppressed, isolated or eliminated. The subtler and more scientific approaches of education, contraception, sterilization, and abortion were more practical and acceptable ways to ease the pressures of the alleged overpopulation. Many people in power today have the same beliefs and agenda as Thomas Malthus and Margaret Sanger.

From 1917 to 1928, Margaret Sanger published *Birth Control Review*. In the October 1921 edition, she posted "The Eugenic Value of Birth Control Propaganda." Ms. Sanger's words show her views on eugenics and birth control in the black community.

In many of her letters, she espoused the ideas of eugenics and classified people into categories of who should live and have children and who shouldn't. Many of her letters express her ideas and her support of the Malthus theory.

Adolph Hitler in his idea of the Aryan race and ridding the world of the unfit or inferior race appears to have adopted ideas from Margaret Sanger and Thomas Malthus. He believed the Aryan race idea was the superior race. However, numerous scholars, including Franz Boas—a nineteenth-century German-American anthropologist and pioneer of modern anthropology—refuted this notion. Boas was awarded a doctorate in 1881 in physics while also studying geography. Aryanism gets its name from prehistoric people who settled in ancient Iran and the northern Indian subcontinents. They spoke Indo-European, especially Germanic, language.

Ms. Sanger spoke about the need to prevent the spread of bad stock. She was actually speaking of the black race and the extremely poor in society. She spoke about the need for birth control and the eugenic value it would provide. Margaret Sanger definitely was an advocate of birth control and wanted to use it as a way to balance the birth rate between the fit and unfit, as she called it. Her goal was to get rid of what she and her followers termed the inferior classes. These so-called classes included poor, mentally ill, and feeble-minded people. She felt it urgent to discourage fertility in these groups and to prevent their propagation.

Margaret Sanger started the Negro Project in 1939. She wrote to Clarence Gamble:

> While the colored Negroes have great respect for the white doctors they can get closer to their own members, we can train the Negro doctor at the clinic, which will have far-reaching results among the colored people.

While Ms. Sanger and her group used the black doctors to convince the Negro people to use birth control, they also used the black ministers and community leaders of that day to reach the people with the same message. The objective was to control the Negro population.

Margaret Sanger and her followers gathered support from segments in black communities. Many prominent black leaders embraced Ms. Sanger's ideas.

While conditions in black communities were already bad, it seemed easy and right among some black leaders to embrace the idea of not bringing more children into a society that worked against them. The idea of making future situations easier for their race was tempting, and often felt worthy of consideration, but people should stop at the door of extermination and not being allowed to exist or increase in numbers.

The human race often finds out later that what was perceived as a good idea when it was sold to them contained ulterior motives. The black condition in America was already bad to say the least, and the idea of not bringing more children into that society had to be appealing to some black leaders. The ulterior motives were to destroy the black population and keep it from increasing and integrating into white society, which would diminish the so-called superior race. Ms. Sanger pushed the idea of the birth control pill in the black community to control population growth—even though it spread throughout the world as a way of controlling how many children a woman could have and when she wanted to have them. Those who believe in eugenics have pushed the idea of overpopulation and insufficient food production. This theory, which has become a scare tactic, has emerged throughout man's existence.

Many seem to act as if education and accumulated knowledge gives them the ability to determine what's best for everyone else or what's best for the world. Some even act as if they know better than God who created human beings and told them to be fruitful and multiply to fill the earth. Are we ignorant enough to think that God didn't know that we would not become overpopulated?

In euthanasia, we have humans often attempting to play God by deciding who should live or die. What makes one individual think that he or she has the right to choose who should be allowed to reproduce or who should be sterile? We all have the right to exist.

When people outgrow a certain area, they branch out and start to build and establish new communities.

God has given us more than enough land to support our living spaces. He has given us more than enough mineral resources to sustain us. If we run out of one mineral, God has given people the intelligence to discover other resources in the earth, which God supplied.

Even in the days of Abraham, God started a nation with one man and one woman. He blessed them and instructed them to be fruitful. This family grew from two people into seventy as they entered Egypt; 430 years later, they had grown into 600,000 men. Including women and children, they probably numbered around three million. God then led them out of Egypt through Moses's leadership and gave them their own land, country, and nation.

When people fear population growth, they begin to institute plans for genocide and euthanasia to kill off segments of society. They identify those they feel are not worthy to live in an effort to control the population. They fear that their survival is somehow threatened by someone else's existence. We all have the right to exist, and God gave us that right.

In 2013 in Virginia, a billboard was installed on the 1700 block of Chamberlayne Avenue. "We need your help to reclaim education and stop the Negro Project" When it was noticed, it generated much controversy because of the language. Many black people thought the sign was offensive, but they had never heard about the Negro Project.

Many people don't know that the Negro Project was set up by Margaret Sanger and others who espoused her views. They wanted to limit the regeneration of black people and those they deemed unfit for society.

The Virginia Christian Alliance installed the sign with good intentions. Their hope was to educate people, especially black people, about the abortion rate in the black community. The sign was taken down on September 13, 2013, but another sign went up in its place. Also two other signs—on West Cary Street and Nine Mile Road—said, "History calls it the 'Negro Project.' Our community needs to know now. Please attend!"

Terry Beatley, the spokesperson for the Virginia Christian Alliance, said,

"Those billboards are a sincere invitation to anybody who wants to come out and learn the truth about the Negro Project. It is not a racist statement. It's actually just the opposite." Mrs. Beatley made reference to Margaret Sanger's 1939 Negro Project, calling it a devious way to reduce the black population through abortion. The Virginia Christian Alliance is a creationist, pro-life, pro-abstinence-only, antigay religious organization. With all the groups in America espouses their views as rights, this Christian group should be allowed to express their views as well.

Abortion rates among blacks rank higher than other races. Many don't realize this. Especially those in the black community. Churches and clergy need to understand what the Negro Project was all about and began teaching young men and women the importance of abstinence, which will reduce the amount of unwanted pregnancies.

In December 2013, the CDC reported that nearly 36 percent of all abortions performed between 2007 and 2010 were in the black community, and black people make up approximately 13 percent of the nation's population.

Hispanics recorded 21 percent of abortions, and it was 7 percent for other minority races. The abortion rate among whites declined about 3 percent during that period. In 2012, there were 31,000 abortions among black women in New York, which were 6,700 more abortions than births. For years, pro-life supporters have attempted to point out the high rate of abortions among black people. They've pointed out that black people and other minorities are being targeted for abortion services.

Considering the abortion rate among black people, it's estimated that millions of babies are being aborted in black communities. Approximately 1,900 black babies are aborted each day in America. It is estimated that 79 percent of Planned Parenthood facilities are located in minority communities. Margaret Sanger was the founder of Planned Parenthood; almost fifty years after her death, her goal for black genocide is working out as she planned.

People's rights are not being forcibly taken; they are taken cunningly and craftily through legislation and social programs that appear to be a good thing on the surface but have devastating ulterior motives. This type of genocide is done through the art of persuasion to get people to kill off their own offspring in masses before they are even born. All babies have a right to exist as much as other human beings.

We should go back to the source of the problem. Margaret Sanger and others encouraged black doctors, preachers, and community leaders to persuade their people to have abortions. Because of that encouragement, the abortion rate in the black community has skyrocketed. Doctors have a responsibility to inform their patients about the effects abortions, including higher risks of breast and ovarian cancer. Community leaders should inform their communities that easy abortion in the black community is a ploy to control black population growth.

The black preachers in their pulpits should preach the Word of God as is it written and inform people that sex outside of marriage, which is defined as fornication is wrong in the eyes of God as well as frown on. Many references in the Bible show God's feelings and his judgment about this practice. Marriage should be preached and taught greatly in churches until the message takes effect—and changes begin to take place in black communities. There will be an increase in the marriage rate among black people and a decrease in the divorce rate. Another result would be fewer children being raised without fathers, which should result in more stable individuals for society and more stable relationships in black communities.

Pastors will have to teach the proper concepts of marriage and parental responsibility. The Pew Institute lists blacks as the most religious race in America, topping at 87% in their 2007 survey on religious affiliation in America. With this percentage, black pastors have a unique opportunity to reach people on these issues. It should be taught that the family is the greatest institution in the world—as well as being the first one. God ordained the family after the creation of the first family (Adam and Eve).

The church should teach that abortion is wrong in the eyes of God by using Jeremiah 1:5, Psalm 139:13, and other scriptures.

Abstinence should be taught in the church because it is a biblical concept, and parents should reinforce this idea to their children at home. Abortion has become a source of birth control for many, especially in black communities. Black babies also have a right to exist.

Chapter 4

The Rights of the Jewish People to Exist

W ho came up with the idea of Israel's right to exist? Why is there such hatred for such a small nation, that its existence is constantly schemed and plotted against? God created the Israelis before many of its enemy nations was formed. Among nations, America has been instrumental in helping Israel maintain its right to exist. This American policy passes from one president to the next—regardless of political party.

The Jewish nation started with Abraham, his wife Sarah, and their son Isaac. Isaac had twin sons, and God chose the younger, Jacob, for the promise of building a nation. God later changed to Jacob's name to Israel, which means power with God. Israel had twelve sons, which became the twelve tribes or families of Israel. Each son represented a tribe, and each tribe was given a portion of land in Canaan, which is now called Palestine.

The hatred for Israel started with the descendants of Jacob's brother Esau. Their nation was known as Edom. The first recorded instance of their hatred for their chosen brethren was when Israel made its exodus from Egypt under the leadership of Moses and needed to pass through Edom of which they refused. Jacob and Esau had long ago made amends and reconciled their differences, but Esau's descendants would not let the hatred die. They knew that Esau was the older son of Isaac, and by natural rights, he should have obtained the inheritance. However, God ordained that the younger son would rule over the elder, and he chose Jacob over Esau for the inheritance.

Edom felt that they had as much right to the blessings of Abraham as Jacob or Israel. Even the offspring of Abraham (through his son Ishmael) wanted to claim rights to the blessings of Abraham. The fight went on from generation to generation and continues to this day. God promised and gave Israel the land from Lebanon or the Nile River to the Euphrates River. Because Israel refused to keep its part of the covenant with God, they lost their land again and again throughout the years. There were numerous attempts to wipe them from the face of the earth, but God continued to be with them, in spite of their disobedience, allowing their seed to remain.

Many question the right of the Jewish people to exist or dwell in their native homeland, although at the present time, it is mostly occupied by Muslims. It is evident that it is their native land from many signs and archeology. After being conquered by Rome in AD 70, a sign remains that it is the Jew's native land. At the Wailing Wall, Jews assemble and pray on a regular basis, inserting prayers on small pieces of paper between the cracks.

In 1948, the United Nations created the modern state of Israel by dividing Palatine. One state was established for the Jewish residents, and the other was for its Arab residents. Great Britain had previously controlled the land of Israel after defeating the Ottoman Empire. The Jews began resettling in the land of Palestine as early as the late 1800s because of oppression and persecution in Europe. However, there remained a remnant (as the Bible calls it) of Jews in the land after the destruction of the temple in AD 70.

After Israel's establishment, David Ben-Gurion made the official announcement on May 15, 1948. On the same day, Arab nations attacked Israel, including forces from Egypt, Syria, Lebanon, Iraq, and Jordan. Israel prevailed, and most of the attacking countries remain enemies of Israel. Israel also gained additional land during the war. Israel has prevailed in all the attacks against them—whether they were spiritual or physical—and they prevailed because God was and is with them. God defending them and fighting for them has been their heritage, keeping them in existence. Prior to the war, Israel had pleaded for peace with its neighbors, but it was rejected.

Nineteenth-century French philosopher Ernest Renan wrote an essay entitled "What Is a Nation?" that helped popularize the phrase "Israel's right to exist." Israel's right to exist has become a popular phrase in Arab-Israeli conflicts. The surrounding nations feel that they have the right to occupy land in Palestine, and Israel claims a God-given right to the land. America had supported Israel's right to the land and has been an ally since 1948.

On June 5, 1967, Arabs who were supported by Egypt, Syria, and Jordan attacked Israel. The Six-Day War lasted until June 10. The Arab states, though larger in numbers, suffered more casualties (twenty thousand) than Israel did (one thousand). Israel obtained control of the West Bank, the Gaza Strip, and the Sinai Desert.

Israel has been defending itself since that time, and its defense system is second to none. The Iron Dome intercepts and destroys short-range rockets directed toward Israel and other artillery fired from up to forty-five miles away. The Iron Dome protects civilian areas that are in the path of enemy attacks.

The war against Israel continues in the hearts of Arab nations, but they are hated by other nations too. Russia, Great Britain, and other nations seem to have disgust for Israel as well, launching verbal attacks or physical attacks against them and challenging their right to existence. For many years, under the leadership of Yasser Arafat, Palestine kept conflicts going with Israel. Mr. Arafat vowed to destroy Israel and kill all Jews. Egypt, Saudi Arabia, Iraq, and Iran supported him.

In 1973, Arab armies again attacked Israel. Syria and Egypt led the attack; Iraq, Libya, Saudi Arabia, Kuwait, and five other countries lent military support. Just as before, Israel defeated the forces.

When Menachem Begin became prime minister of Israel in 1977, he said, "We were granted our right to exist by the God of our fathers at the glimmer of the dawn of human civilization four thousand years ago."

This could not have been spoken any better. Here it is now 2015, we have the first black president in the White House—something that American society, especially its black citizens, thought would never happen—and we continue to hear this phrase of Israel's right to exist.

They have the right to exist because—as the prime minister stated—God gave it to them. Who ever heard of such a thing? People are arrogant enough to try to play God and say who can exist or live and who cannot. All of this is done under the guise of *rights*. Everyone is a direct descendent of one man and one woman, Adam and Eve, who God created. Israel has the right to exist just as much as any other nation or people.

In every attempt to destroy the Jews, they still exist because God is with them. Even though Israel is a state, Israel is also the Jewish people—and they are a nation as well. There may be many other attempts to annihilate them, but because God is with them and for them, they will prevail and continue to exist. They have been attacked in their homeland, but they have a right to it.

In other nations with large Jewish populations, Israel's existence has also been threatened. The most recognized was Adolph Hitler and Germany's genocide of the Jewish people. Hitler and the German people were prejudiced against Jews and other races. They thought they were superior and wanted to create a superior race while exterminating the so-called inferior ones. Their idea of the superior race was white skin, blond hair, and blue eyes. Not all Germans supported Adolf Hitler's views, just as all white people were not in favor of slavery and other injustices in the United States. People who didn't agree with Hitler were executed or thrown into prison camps. Hitler instructed his soldiers to "have no pity and act brutally!"

Adolf Hitler persecuted the Jewish people and ordered them to be killed in countries he controlled. He set up concentration camps, and an estimated three million Jews were murdered in Germany alone. His forces killed about six million European Jews and approximately five million other people he considered racially inferior or politically dangerous. He had the natural power, and in his mind, they had no right to exist. Nobody has the power to make such decisions like that besides God, who is the creator of all the races. Every race has a God-given right to exist. No one should have the power to exterminate a race of people because he or she feels they shouldn't exist.

On March 26, 1979 the first peace treaty between Israel and an Arab country was signed in Washington, DC, ending Egypt's fight against Israel. The treaty was signed by Anwar El Sadat, president of

Egypt and Israeli Prime Minister Menachem Begin. The agreements became known as the Camp David Accords because the negotiations took place at the US presidential retreat at Camp David, Maryland, and were sponsored by President Jimmy Carter. President Sadat and Prime Minister Begin were awarded the Nobel Prize for Peace in 1978 for their contributions to the agreements. Since 1948, Israel wanted to live in peace with its neighbors, but its Arab neighbors refused to accept them as a nation and attacked them continually.

Israel has the same right to exist as any other nation. One couldn't help but wonder, why they appear to be hated so, that their existence is threatened by so many. Why are they such a hated people? Could it be because they are God's chosen people? Whose right is right—the nations that want Israel's destruction or Israel, which continues to fight for its right to exist?

It is appalling that a sovereign nation's right to exist can be questioned. They exist, and they have a God-given right to exist. To deny Israel's right to exist is to deny the existence of God. For many years, the United States, who has been an ally of Israel, has provided them with foreign aid, military support, and diplomatic support.

The United States was probably the first sovereign nation to recognize Israel as a state. Despite tension between President Barack Obama and Israeli Prime Minister Benjamin Netanyahu, America continues to be supportive of Israel and its right to exist. This has been American policy since 1948.

In 1967, Soviet Union premier Alexei Kosygin asked President Lyndon B. Johnson why America was so adamant about supporting Israel. The president explained that it was the right thing to do. Israel is the means whereby God used a people to bring a Savior to the world. Christians recognize that Israel is the key to the return of the Savior

Not recognizing or accepting Israel's right to exist threatens the rights of us all. Today it is an attack against Israel, but tomorrow, it could be America. Whose right is right—ours in support of Israel's right to exist or others who want Israel's destruction? As stated in the beginning, whose rights are right?